The Big Mountain Diaries

Summer Crystalcrow

Author: Summer Crystalcrow

First published in 2014

Text and illustration copyright © 2014 Julia Orr

Cover design: Debbie Spafford

ISBN: 978-0-9904245-0-5

Library of Congress: 2014910718

All Rights Reserved.

This novel is a work of fiction. Names and characters are the product of the author's imagination and any resemblance to actual persons, living or dead, is entirely coincidental.

No part of this publication may be reproduced, stored in a retrieval system or transmitted by any form or by any means, electronic, recording or otherwise without the prior permission in writing from the publishers.

Unauthorised reproduction of any part of this publication by any means including photocopying is an infringement of copyright.

Contents

	Acknowledgements
	Introduction
I.	City Indian
II.	The Beginning
III.	Up on Big Mountain – Christmas 1998
IV.	January, 1999
V.	February 5 – 7, 1999
VI.	Gathering of Nations
VII.	Gaia Communications Run – March 5, 1999
VIII.	The Alders Weekend
IX.	May 1, 1999
X.	June 19, 1999
XI.	June 25 run
XII.	August 1, 1999
XIII.	August 7, 1999
XIV.	Animal Abuse Report, August 1999
XV.	September 9, 1999
XVI.	October 22, 1999
XVII.	Christmas Run of 1999
XVIII.	Relocation Deadline, January 27, 2000
XIX.	January 28, 2000
XX.	January 29, 2000
XXI.	January 30, 2000
XXII.	January 31, 2000
XXIII.	February 1, 2000
XXIV.	February 2, 2000
XXV.	February 3, 2000
XXVI.	The Ill Fated Thanksgiving Run, 2000
XXVII.	For The Love of The Earth

Acknowledgements

I felt called to write this book because it seemed to me the magic of the world was fading. The overwhelming destruction of our precious planet seemed as a tidal wave, and I wanted to tell the story of some of the most beautiful peoples I had the privilege of meeting. And, in some small way acknowledge how the indigenous tribes have warned us, how they have been warning us for years, and we continue to ignore them determined to have "scientific" proof before we put the care of the Earth and her creatures before our rapacious desire for money. Undoubtedly, without meeting the dragon man, Rory James, and being enchanted by his connection to Native Americans I would never have set foot on this path. Thanks also to Gregory Butler who insisted I go and meet his crazy writer friend who hooked me up with my first sweatlodge ceremony. Serendipitous indeed. There are no words of gratitude deep enough to thank Ben Spirithorse and his family for all they have been to me and for all of the adventures we have been on together. This story would never have been told without him. Thanks to my dear friend and co-driver Muriel Vernon who first encouraged me to write this book and made such a wonderful companion on many trips. To all of my co-drivers, Stefan, Erica Hamilton and Steph. Special thanks to Stefan who was kind enough to edit the first copy of my draft. To wolf man Vic.

How does one thank all of the Dineh and Hopi who are this story? There really are no words to express the gratitude I feel to have met each and every one I cannot name, and thank for all they shared with me. To my soul sister, Snowdeer who passed way too early from this world and without whom I would never have known such magic existed. To my peeps in London who host me and keep me going with their wonderful friendship; Becca, Gary, Minnie-Mae, Ellery, Atlanta and Mark and the kids, Beresford, Spencer and Lola. A special thanks to Stump, Julie and Ruby Rose whom have my admiration always. Last but not least, thanks to my family, Chris, Kirsty, Layla, Leo, Paula, Adie, Amelia, Peter, Noelle and Michaela and especially my loving father who always encouraged my adventures, and to my dear, dear mum, who ignited the love of books and writing in me.

Introduction

As each of us sits in the circle and engages in the fire dance of life, the flames appear differently to each set of eyes. This makes up the individuals experience of the string of events which IS our lives. One of our greatest challenges is to celebrate these differences.

That said, these journals are my story from my own personal view of a journey I shared with many. Each of those people will have a different version of this tale, and that is what colors us the people we are. My story is not the whole truth in its entirety of the events depicted, it is merely a part of it. Many others shared the same path and had their own experience, no view being lesser or greater than the others, just unique as we all are.

I did not want to color this journey with rose tinted spectacles and portray everyone as having a perfectly lovely time, because that was not how it was. It was always gritty, difficult, stressfull and demanding in more ways than I knew there were but with plenty of beauty, love, fun and adventure thrown in. I also did not want to depict myself or the people involved as wonderful people having the greatest of adventures. The truth is that everybody has their shadow selves, myself included. My continuous search is for truth. There were always drama, ego and personality clashes to contend with. I kept the diaries pretty much as I wrote them at the time, I share what I saw, felt and heard at the time I experienced it.

I do not speak for or represent either the Hopi or Dineh people, and I do not tell their story as that is not mine to tell. I pass on what was shared with me and the reasons that called me out to the land, a place that led all of us to shed vast amounts of tears. My heart still hurts when I think of the environmental devastation that continues on Big Mountain to this day and beyond. To finally know what it is to be one with all life is to know the suffering of it all too. Even if my life's path never leads me there again, she still speaks to me in my dreams. I will always be connected to Big Mountain, as in the grande words of the song: "I am Her, She is Me, and We are One."

During the time I spent supporting the Dineh resistance there was in effect a media blackout. Some brave souls were interested enough to bypass that censorship and do a story on the relocation issues. But somehow it never received its due attention and we, as a group, finally exhausted all the possibilities we had. Maybe some who read this will be energized enough to renew support for the resisting elders, the few that are left, and that would be blessing enough and the reason for this story to be told. I doubt not that this will reignite some forgotten feelings, not all of which will be good. And, as always with Big Mountain issues, I expect there will be people with negative opinions on my actions – ah the drama! There are, of course, people out there who played a much larger part then mine and who were, and are still, much more involved. Maybe this will encourage them to tell their own story so we all may benefit from the richness that was and is blessed in their lives.

Who would have thought that by bringing society fossil fuel electricity to power people's lives, other people would be subject to abuse, torture, and even their very lives would be forfeit to protect the corporations? So, of course, all names herein are fictional to protect those who would suffer from victimization from the people the Hopi refer to as "the two hearted."

To all my relations and ancestors above, below, and beyond. Especially to ALL the animals, who silently bring us help and magic to guide our way, expecting no thanks in return, just begging that one day we will wake up to their sacredness and stop their daily slaughter.

I remember the parts of the Hopi prophecy that stick in my mind the most and am reminded of them on a daily basis, the part about that many will die and the part about how there will be dead people walking around. I see it now. It is no longer prophecy.

Summer Crystal Crow

Chief Dan Evehema's message to mankind

"So many people have come to Hopiland to meet with us. Some of you we have met on your lands. Many times people have asked how they can help us. Now I hope and pray that your help will come. If you have a way to spread the truth, through the newspapers, radio, books through meeting with powerful people, tell the truth! Tell them what you know to be true. Tell them what you have seen here; what you heard us say; what you have seen with your own eyes. In this way if we do fall, let it be said that we tried, right up to the end, to hold fast to the path of peace as we were orginally instructed to do by the Great Spirit."

Chief Dan Evehema, (105) Spriritual leader, Eldest Elder Greeswood/Roadrunner Clan Society Father/Snake Priest/Kachina Father

Hotevilla, Arizona

I

City Indian

I knew from the first moment I laid eyes on Rory James that someone had just walked in through the door who would change my life forever. It was more all encompassing than love at first sight, it was more like love at first strike, and that filled me with such fear I could barely speak. The door, unceremoniously, just happened to be the door of the liquor store, around the corner from my friend Tim's house in Maida Vale, London. The liquor store in England is called the "Off Licence" or more commonly known as the "Offi." The English have a penchant for playing with their words to make a stylized street language it was doubtful any tourist would understand.

Perhaps that was the point of it; England was a mixing bowl of ethnicities by the late 80s. It was as if growing up English you just had to mutate the language into a modern day cockney rhyming slang. The strange part about it was, most of your friends completely understood you but outsiders were just baffled, much to everyone's amusement. That Friday night, like every Friday night, was party night. The English, they say, could find any excuse to drink, but that night was special. That Friday night was New Year's Eve, and many arrangements had to be made to ensure a perfect party. The most important was the mad cocktail of drugs and alcohol that was required during the hedonistic 90s to ensure a good time was had by all.

I can still hear the jangle of the bell above the door of the Offi as it opened, like an alarm bell from Heaven. It was one of those old-fashioned types that left the actual bell part jiggling madly with each new customer passing through. And I can still feel the overwhelming emotions that rose inside of me like a tsunami as I watched a precocious city Indian saunter into the store as if life itself amused him. Years later those emotions still threaten to make a fairground ride out of my stomach when I think about it. Richard Butler, my partner in crime for the night and a very dear friend, was talking to me, but I was momentarily lost until a sharp rebuke from him to pay attention snapped me back to the present. I tried to look as if nothing had happened as if my mind had momentarily wandered, but he knew me better than that and his piercing gaze searched my face for clues. I couldn't stand the scrutiny as he looked around the shop for whatever had caught my attention and as the Ferris wheel in my stomach lurched into high speed I flung the money at the Pakistani shop owner who was standing watching us with nervous anxiety.

"What's the matter?" Richard asked as he peered around the shop, "What were you looking at?" Richard's face resembled that of a bird. Long sharp nose, small very dark eyes, and his mind was as sharp as a hunting bird of prey.

"Let's get out of here before trouble finds me," I replied. Clutching our valuable party favours for the night, I fled the store with Richard in tow, hoping that the universe was not snapping at my heels demanding I fall into the abyss of whatever lesson that was going to be, but indeed it did. As I later found out there was no escape, and I was not going to be let off very easily. The turn of events that night became the gauge that led the train of my life down a very different track.

By chance or not, the city Indian was going to the same party as Richard and I. I remember my eyes growing wide with alarm and my mind panicking as soon as he walked into the room. It was very confusing as I couldn't really understand what was bothering me so much: all I had to do was avoid a stranger, so why was my entire being freaking out? All of the atoms in my body seem to be doing a war dance with the universe, which in turn was making the sparks fly in my brain as if it were trying to kick start a motorbike I had been quietly anesthetizing with dope since my teens.

I spent a good deal of the time at the party leaving each room as Rory James entered so I could try to avoid what was quickly turning into an overwhelming physical attraction for him. Not good for me, particularly as I didn't have the best reputation when it comes to men, being quite addicted to the delectables of the male body, and I habitually and avariciously indulged my appetite. As it turned out, Rory was quite well known at the party by mutual friends. Tim, Roland and an upcoming actor, Sean Pertwee – the son of the late Dr. Who, John Pertwee and Rory had all grown up together. Rory's father had died when he was young, so after that, as happens with most fatherless boys, he became a notorious trouble maker who liked to live on the wilder side of life. He even dressed like the gangster rappas did, baggy pants, large baseball styled jacket and baseball cap. Even his clothes were slightly unique. Later, I found out he designed them himself and that was the trade he wanted to break into. At that time though, he was best known for being a drug dealer and to me he spelt danger in huge flashing neon letters. This one would be worse than "Lost in Space" I thought. This time, I would not get out of whatever experience the Great Teacher of the universe was planning for me with my heart in one piece. Unfortunately for me, the unseen powers that be seemed to be indulging themselves in being a fiendishly brilliant coordinator. As deftly as I avoided Rory James they, as deftly, connived to get us together.

I had sequestered myself in the corner of the living room with my girlfriend, Audrey Brown. We were chatting and getting more stoned by the moment with our backs to the rest of the room as if to indicate we wanted to be left alone to speak privately. But then, for some unknown reason, she turned her head and spotted my city Indian walking into the room. Before I could make a gracious exit she had shouted,

"Hey Rory, come over here and meet Summer." And with a mad twinkle in her eye turned to me and said, "You are perfect for each other, you can just fuck each other and leave!" As my insides screamed, "Escape, escape Will Robinson!" the stranger, whom I had obsessively tried to avoid without knowing why, seated himself next to me and proceeded to ask what I was into. "Excellent," I thought as I saw an opportunity to become completely boring in the hopes he would get up and leave,

"Books," I said tritely, expecting that to be the last thing he would find interesting, "I read a lot." I hoped that if I projected a stuffy librarian image he would take fright and leave. But of course the universe has a great sense of humour and doesn't take no for an answer. I was hopelessly lost to his charms from the moment Rory James replied,

"Oh excellent, I love books, better than all these boring fucks at this party too out of it on Ecstasy to have anything interesting to say."

For the rest of the night we sat and talked, and it was these words Rory spoke I will always remember because it was these seemingly innocent words that instigated a huge change in my life and set me on a totally unexpected path.

"If you really want to know who I am," which of course, I did, "I'll take you to see the directors cut of "Dances with Wolves," and there is a line in that film where he says, 'I am Wind In His Hair and I will always be your friend.' If you recognize that part, you will know where I am coming from." He spoke each word deliberatly and clearly, as if to make sure I had understood him fully. He emphazised the part about recognizing the line as if this was a clue to unlocking the mystery that was Rory James. How gloriously dramatic and kind of geeky, like a bad trailer from "Gone with the Wind," but needless to say I fully intended to see the film as I hadn't yet anyway. Because now I was hooked and quite willing to surrender my heart to this unique and dangerous soul regardless of the consequences.

Again the universe stepped in to take care of the next arrangement through the kind courtesy of Audrey, who sat there grinning throughout the entire exchange.

"Summer, Rory was looking for a ride home. You can get a taxi together! Couldn't he crash at your place until the tube starts?" And into the web I had gone, wrapped and bound.

"Yes!" I heard myself say, "Yes, you can do that if you want." And that was that. I left with the dangerous, yet utterly unavoidable man.

We called a taxi and headed back to Camden Town where I lived with my gay roommate, Michael, in the attic of a tall Victorian house painted stark white against the cold grey that is always London. My flat overlooked a crescent shaped park surrounded by tall trees. From the windows, you could only see the tops of the trees with the odd chimney pot poking up in the distance, which gave the impression you lived amidst abundant woodland. It belied the fact a main artery for London traffic ran on the other side of the small park, and the noise of cars was a constant thrum throughout the day and night. At around 3 a.m the noise would stop for about an hour, and then start up again with the morning onslaught of cars. This had been incredibly annoying to me when I first moved into the flat but after a while I barely noticed it. It was only when someone new came around and stayed the night that it would come up again in conversation. The outstide of the house was impressive, with pillars standing guard outside the front door. Iron railings ran the length of the crescent of houses, a rarity to find any that had survived the confiscation of iron during the Second World War. I opened the door half expecting to see my landlady who lived in the front room of the ground floor. She had an ever watchful eye on the comings and goings on of the tenants in her house. Her husband, a small grey immigrant from Greece, lived in the back kitchen and whenever I went to pay my rent he was always dressed in striped pyjamas cooking eggs and listening to the radio. I don't think Betty and her husband had spoken in years, and appeared to spend separate lives in the front and back of the house. There were four levels to the old house and no lift, so you had to climb the stairs which was quite the work-out if you weren't used to it or carrying heavy shopping. The stair carpet always made me laugh. It was a kind of 70's pattern. Anything you dropped on it would disappear into the mad chocolate brown and orange swirls of design never to be found again, except perhaps by the vacuum cleaner that was run over the stairs once in a blue moon.

Rory and I climbed those stairs together, and I grew more anxious with every step. His face revealed nothing but that slight amusement at life, his Mona Lisa smile. When we finally made it up to my attic flat, I made tea for us, an English tradition. Nothing happens in England without drinking tea first.

Hot, milky and sweet. As we sat on the couch, I explained to him in my best serious manner that we were to be just friends and be adults about him staying the night. We could share my single bed but nothing was to happen, it was just a case of keeping each other cozy and warm because the couch wasn't really big enough for anyone to sleep on. Rory nodded and smiled, neither objecting or agreeing, but everything was fine by him. Somehow, of course we both knew it wasn't going to happen like that. It seemed to be my last final ridiculous attempt at ordering the pace of this relationship. I changed into PJ's and slid into my narrow bed to watch Rory. He sat on the bed and looked at me and jokingly said,

"Now don't get all weird will you when I undress." I didn't quite know what he meant but replied,

"Oh please!" in a sarcastic manner. As I watched, he took off his bulky blue corduroy jacket and then his baseball cap. My eyes bulged as he unwound a long coil of hair that had been hidden under his baseball cap. The sides of his head were shaved so you couldn't see he had long hair . He shook it loose and it fell invitingly down his back. As he pulled up his shirt to bare his chest, I openly gasped,

"Oh my god." Tattooed over each shoulder coiled large dragons, vivid in their intricacy, emerald colored with blazing red eyes. Before my eyes, Rory James had turned from a dope dealing street hustler into a mythical warrior resplendant in his skin. I smiled, ah the universe is never wrong!

A few weeks later we did go to see the film, "Dances with Wolves." We sat in the back of the cinema and Rory rolled a huge spliff. Perhaps that's what did it. My heart burned with recognition, but I knew not of what. Of course, I remembered what he had said and when it appeared in the film; I even understood where this lost boy was coming from. And so I spent nearly a year in a crazy affair with Rory James whom I jokingly called the bag man for the huge bag of clothes he had designed himself, and which he would carry with him everywhere to sell in Camden Market. I never had his phone number, and I never knew where he lived, just that it was somewhere in North London. He had to remain fairly incognito because of some bad deal he had done somewhere that had gone wrong and now he had enemies. It was all very mysterious and vague. Rory would just turn up on a Friday evening and I always knew when he was going to call. It was as if I could feel when he was near. Our time together was spent indulging in the typical mad London night life until, like another cliché, the phone call came that truly changed my life.

An Irish friend of mine had gotten married to an American animator and had moved to Los Angeles. She was lonely and had persuaded him to get the studio he worked for to hire me to head up their animation checking department. The movie they were making, an animated film called 'Bebe's Kids', was in schedule hell and they needed someone who was experienced enough to help deliver it on time. Amazingly enough, that was where I came in to the picture. It was a great offer, but then there was Rory. I was madly in love with him and didn't want to leave. After days of deliberating, I walked up to where I knew he was working and asked him what I should do. He said, quite simply "Go! Because if it was me, I would go in a flash." And that was that. Now, parts of me still regret that decision. The part that wonders what would have happened if I hadn't left. I know that we would not have lasted as he was just too volatile and in reality he was a key that opened this opportunity for me. The key the universe had sent to me to send me off on the path I was meant to be on, but I still wistfully wonder.

When the day came to leave, the studio in LA sent me a car to take me to the airport which was a luxury I had never previously enjoyed. I dropped Rory off in Camden Market and never really saw him again. I called the mobile number he had eventually given me and tried to stay in touch but as it happened he left the phone in a taxi one night and I had no other way of connecting with him. After four months on the job, I came tearing home exhausted from working all the hours god sent and tired of LA. I wanted to find Rory and eventually tracked him down at a party in North London. But everything in him had changed, and as I pouted and chastized him, he rejected me mysteriously saying, "It was all in your head." To this day I wonder how he knew what fantasies I had in my head about him. I never spoke about it, made sure never to mention any future plans or anything that would not have been cool. I think his best friend, whose name I can't even remember now, played a large part in our dissolution. Rory admired him enormously, probably looked up to him as a father figure having lost his when he was very young, but this guy was a heroin addict who probably had nothing else in his life but Rory. I've never met a heroin addict that was anything but selfish and consumed by the addiction, so I believe that if he had seen any hint in Rory of moving on with a woman, or of being happy, he would have squashed that immediately. People have a habit of wanting to spread their misery.

It wasn't until the next year when I was invited back to LA to work on another animated film, that things really started changing in a big way. Rory's influence had turned me on to the Native American life. He was always talking about how he would love to do a sweat lodge ceremony, Sundance, or take peyote. Of course, in my naivete I thought that the Indian way of life was gone. That we had massacred it in our quest for expansion, but I was wrong. The first real job I had in LA, even though I had barely enough time to eat and sleep, I managed to read a part of "Bury my Heart at Wounded Knee" every day, and I cried rivers of tears over it.

After the film was finished I returned home to England and my small flat in Camden Town. One day, about a year after Rory had left my life, I had a call from an American friend who insisted I go and meet a lady friend of his in Camden Lock. He told me she had participated in a sweat lodge ceremonies in LA, and had a contact for me for whenever I went back and wanted to go to one. We arranged to meet on Saturday morning and I grumbled all the way. I was not a morning person and Camden Market on a weekend is a nightmare, packed with tourists and Saturday shoppers. I never usually ventured up there at the weekend, but I went and met this crazy scattered American who turned out to be an author. She gave me the number for a contact in LA who could tell me where a sweat lodge ceremony was being conducted on a regular basis.

I had no plans to return to LA at that time, but funnily enough, the universe took care of that arrangement again. Within the next few months, I was, surprisingly to me, back in LA after getting another animation job with Hanna Barbera through an American friend who had also just recently moved to LA for work. Once I had settled in, I called the number the crazy author had given me for the Sweat Lodge ceremony and spoke to a lady called Star who gave me directions to the land the ceremony was to be held on. The ceremony was taking place in the Malibu Hills on a Monday night, which was at least an hours journey in good traffic. So I persuaded the guy I was dating at the time to come with me, and it turned out to be a most frustrating journey. That night the freeway was packed, and I was getting more and more irritated by the minute. My boyfriend had picked me up late and then we had to stop to get the supplies we had been asked to bring, namely bottled water and tobacco. It was again all very mysterious, but with a burning desire in my heart, and perhaps a small part of me wanting to find Rory again in this adventure, we took off. The land where the ceremony was being held was at the top of the mountain. The actual place was very hard to find in the dark, and as we wove our way up the mountain road, I peered through the darkness trying to spot the turnoff, which apparently was not particularly marked by anything but a small red flag.

After driving past it once and having to backtrack, which irritated me no end, we eventually found the dirt track turnoff and drove through a narrow passage of sandstone hills, which opened up onto a wide swath of land overlooking the Pacific Ocean. There were a bunch of cars parked on the grass, so we followed suit. We could see the glow of the fire flickering against the sandstone bluffs on one side of the land and followed the muffled sound of drumming and chanting. The site seemed to me prehistoric and ancient. The sweatlodge had been built jutting up against the rock formations up on a little ridge, and the fire created dancing shadows on the walls enhancing the magical atmosphere. There was a large firepit containing the stones which would be put inside the hut for heat. The lodge was a low dome-like construction made out of willow, covered in blankets with an entrance facing east. An altar made from the dirt dug from the firepit was between the fire pit and the lodge and was covered with all sorts of bones, stones and feathers.

A sweating man with long black hair tied back with a bandana, the firekeeper, tended the fire and used a pitch fork to carry the stones over to the lodge. New stones were given over to the sweat leader after each round, of which there are traditionally four, one for each direction. I later discovered that each sweatlodge ceremony can be slightly different depending on who is running it. The hardest sweat ceremonies were called warrior sweats, a group of very macho men running it somehow always managed to make the hottest, hardest sweats to get through. I could never tell if it was their energy or if indeed they somehow managed to make the stones hotter.

Not being the most patient of people, I was incredibly annoyed blaming my companion for his tardiness, as the ceremony had already started when we arrived. Luckily, they were used to late new arrivals from Hollywood and so the sweat leader let us in after the first round had finished. We changed into sweat clothes we had been advised to bring, cotton skirt and tee shirt for me, shorts for men, and crawled in through the low mantel of the doorway on hands and knees into an experience that was so out of my understanding that I had zero expectations. I had no clue what I was getting myself into. But knew somehow that I was in the right place for me at this time in my life. Once we were inside the lodge, the ceremony started up again. I sat in the pitch black listening to the drums, the wonderful words of the songs and prayer and my whole life started to transform. It was as if a magical door had opened, never to be closed again. The sweat that was pouring out of me was like the rivers of tears I had refused to shed over Rory. When we were finished and I replenished my body with clean fresh water, I knew that this was all meant to be. Life unfolded.

II

The Beginning

The first time I went out to Big Mountain on the Navajo reservation in Arizona it was Thanksgiving, and I can't even remember what year it was. I had started dating Will Nightshade, one helluva rogue Lakota whom I had recently met through a friend, Ben Spirit Horse, while attending a sweat lodge ceremony. Ben had been running food and supplies up to the Elders of Big Mountain for a few months and had persuaded Will and me to go up to the reservation with him. That weekend we drove Ben's brown jeep while Ben drove his work van with his girlfriend Amy and their baby girl, Mae. There was another activist guy who came with us, and there was Beth from Ojai, who drove up in the VW van she also lived in.

Winter Davis, a homeless outreach activist from LA, and her boyfriend also drove up with us. In fact it had been Winter who had initially discovered what was going on with the Dineh after noticing a lot of homeless guys from the rez turning up in Venice beach. She had decided to try and figure out why that was, took a trip to Arizona and tracked their stories back to the Navajo rez, eventually discovering the struggle the Navajo/Dineh and Hopi tribes had been fighting for years with Peabody Coal and the U.S Government. When I read the history, a history that had been written down by whites and was therefore suspect, I was intrigued as to how the timeline of events could be just coincidental. It didn't seem possible that the Dineh would be allocated a reservation without someone realizing that it was on top of one of the richest deposits of coal and uranium in the U.S. I think that perhaps they did realize this, maybe not the uranium, but you can physically see the coal lying just below the surface. It's clearly visible in the deep canyons cut by ancient water. Coal has been mined since the Industrial Revolution in the early 1800s and even earlier, so there is no reason to believe that it wasn't just a matter of logistics that kept a mining company or the U.S government from extracting the coal earlier from Big Mountain than they did. I expect the difficulties of getting the appropriate equipment to the remote location could have been either the entire or at least partly the reason. Even today most of the reservation is made up of dirt roads, which make travel extremely difficult, if not impassable, without the right vehicle, especially in inclement weather. The Bureau of Indian Affairs (BIA) created the actual reservation in 1882, after the Navajo had been "allowed" to return to their ancestral homeland from Bosque Redondo where they had been relocated previously. The newly designated reservation encompassed the mesas where the Hopi had been living since the migration times as well as the surrounding area of rangeland, which the Dineh occupied. The two tribes had co-existed peacefully since pre Columbus times. Nothing much changed for both tribes, who lived their traditional ways of life for the next 70 years until the mid 1950s when the coal deposit was "discovered." It seems so curious to me that they waited until the 1950s to extract this but what is more curious is that they designated this profitable area as a reservation. Did certain people know that if they let the European immigrants settle there it would be practically impossible to remove them in the future once it was time to mine the resources but knew they could do what they wanted with Indian tribes? These old families, like the Rockefellers, hand down their legacies of greed and exploitation to their heirs. I wondered if this was the case with Peabody and the resource-rich lands of the Four Corners area. Wherever you have a mix of the U.S government, coal companies and Native American tribes the plot becomes extremely complicated with much chicanery.

What we do know is that in 1963, the year I was born, white lawyers seemingly backed by the coal companies, petitioned the U.S. government to partition the land occupied by the Hopi and Navajo tribes. The U.S. designated the area occupied by the Dineh people (Navajo) approximately one million acres, as Joint-Use. This meant that both tribes would share rights to the land and any mining royalties. However, the plan required that all Dineh people living in the Joint-Use area be evicted.

In 1974, the U.S. Congress, concerned over the 1973 oil embargo passed a law mandating that all Dineh be relocated from the area. Twelve thousand Dineh were forcibly relocated to a few thousand acres near Chambers, AZ. The area just happened to be contaminated by the worst radioactive spill in the history of America. Many Dineh were dumped into cities; unable to adapt to a non-traditional way of life became homeless, driven to alcoholism and suicide. Liking the people who ran the relocation program to Nazi's, the director of the program resigned.

A few thousand Dineh families remained on their ancestral land defying twenty-five years of efforts to remove them. The remaining peoples were subject to an aggressive persecution campaign. It became illegal for them to repair their homes or collect firewood. Permits were now needed to keep livestock on which their lives depended. Many sheep, cattle and horses were impounded as the B.I.A sort to reduce herds.

The U.S. government ordered the eviction of the remaining "resistors" in 1996 unless they signed a lease agreement. The lease agreement meant that homesteads and land could not be passed down to the next generation. Under threat of violence and misrepresentation of what the lease actually said, numerous Dineh families signed away their homes and civil rights. The majority of Dineh could not read or write English at that time. Many of the Dineh who refused to sign were vulnerable elders living alone in remote home sites who, with glittering obsidian eyes and shotguns, often faced off against truckloads of armed Marshalls come to either evict them or impound their livestock. This is a very simplistic version of the stage I stepped onto in blissful ignorance.

The journey to Big Mountain was great fun: no mechanical problems, fair weather and plenty of smoke. Will and I were still getting to know each other, so we had plenty to say and laugh about. I hadn't really been on too many road trips, so just getting on the endless American roads, stopping at truck stops to eat bad food and buy cheap sunglasses to look cool was a great adventure to me. I guess I felt a bit of a wild rogue myself, driving off into the unknown with a bunch of spirited activists looking to change the world. Pure adventure. It wasn't until after ten hours of driving when we were finally approaching the mesas that a weird sensation started to kick me in my gut.

At first I put it down to being too stoned, getting too paranoid, and tried to ignore the growing strange sensation in me. We had finally left all the towns and freeways behind and were in open country, heading up to the Hopi mesas to visit with Blue Star in the traditional village of Hotevilla. Blue Star was a young Hopi man Ben had met before who was the son of one of the original Hopi traditionalists. The Hopi traditionalists had resisted the implementation of any kind of modernization in their way of life at Hotevilla, sometimes physically jumping in front of bulldozers that were being used to dig ditches to lay sewage lines and power cables. The traditional Hopi people did not want their village to be modernized and felt this would basically be the beginning of the end of their culture and balanced way of living, but there were some Hopi called "progressives" who did want flushing toilets and electricity to be brought into the villages, and this had caused great division between families. The Hopi Tribal Government was made up of people who had, for the most part, been kidnapped as children from their families and forced to attend white schools far away from their home. This enforced education gave them a different perspective from their traditionalist parents, which started the breaking down of the Hopi culture and lifestyle. All done quite deliberately of course, by the whites, the US government, and Christian missionaries.

I had taken over the driving and was enjoying the view immensely. Flat plains drifted into the horizon as far as the eye could see, looming colossal monuments of earth rose up from the ground looking like ancient standing stones of the past. The sky was an azure blue with light fluffy clouds in the distance and everything was so exciting and new for a city girl from England. Ben had run into trouble with the Hopi rangers on a previous visit and wanted to split the caravan up in an effort to look less conspicuous, a strategy we would use in the future so as not to bring attention to ourselves. We all pulled over to the side of the road to discuss where to meet. Will and

I were going to hang back, bring up the rear guard, and drive in alone, meeting them in Hotevilla. Will said he knew the way and had been there plenty of times, so it was no problem. That was actually the truth. So I don't know what strange spirit took him over next or what he was up to.

Even though we were already incredibly stoned, Will and I lit yet another joint. We were both so stupidly obsessed with the coolness of being with each other and then it hit me, like a huge boulder rolling down hill, right in the solar plexus. I stared out the windscreen through the haze of intoxicating smoke. The mesas loomed on the horizon with a strange, foreboding power that hung heavily in the air. Ben and the rest of the team were disappearing down the endless road leaving me alone with… I turned to look at Will…. leaving me alone with someone I hardly knew! What the hell was I thinking! My mind started to panic crazily. Well, I thought the fact that I was with someone I hardly knew wasn't unusual but something wasn't right. As I watched Will, something about him was changing before my eyes. There was some kind of freaky energy at work here, something that came from the mesas. It could sense us and, in sensing us, it reached out for us. It smelled my sensitivity and I had not thought to protect myself energetically and it was too late now, I was wide open.

Suddenly terrified, I jumped out of the car feeling like I wanted to vomit. It made no sense, and the weed was amplifying whatever was going on. I was stricken with an intense paranoia and thought I was going to get killed. I got back in the car and said straight-faced with all my determination,

"Lets go!" Suddenly, I desperately wanted to catch up with the others and not be alone with Will any longer. He simply replied,

"No," with finality, "we'll wait a while longer." He was sitting in the drivers seat; there was nothing I could do. Will leaned over and kissed me, and my mind screamed endlessly. I was absolutely certain something very bad was going to happen.

Finally, when the rest of the caravan had completely disappeared, and we continued to stare at an empty road for what seemed like ages, Will started the car and we took off. He had stopped speaking or laughing and was now tight lipped and poker faced, I guess I must have been too. I was just glad to be moving in what appeared to be the right direction. We came to a crossroads and turned right. After about twenty minutes of driving, Will realized he had gone the wrong way, so we turned around and drove in the opposite direction. Suddenly, he cranked the wheel hard right and turned off the main road, and started heading down a bumpy dirt track. Suddenly losing all ability to converse normally, my throat just shut down with abject fear. I must have looked like a terrified rabbit caught in headlights at this point. I had no idea where we were, and the road, or rather what amounted to little more than a dirt track as far as I could see, led absolutely nowhere.

Later, when I got to know the route to Hotevilla well, it occurred to me how really odd it was that Will had gotten lost the way he did. He was driving us nowhere fast, and the road to Hotevilla is one of the easiest on the rez to remember. We turned around again, and got back on the main road and continued to drive up the mesa. To my huge relief, Ben suddenly appeared around the corner in the white van like a modern day knight in shining armor. We stopped the vehicles side by side on the road. Ben asked us what had happened to us and said he had been worried the rangers had stopped us. Will just told him that he had forgotten the way and we had gotten lost. Ben looked equally perplexed at this answer. My intense feeling slowly subsided and I put it all down to being too stoned. I was so naïve then, I think about that now and laugh.

Hotevilla is a village unlike any I had ever seen before: ancient, mysterious, powerful and simple in design. It sits precariously on the edge of the mesa seemingly so integrated with the mountain you can barely make it out from a distance. The houses are low, square adobe buildings built close together. The traditionalist Hopi, Yukioma, and his followers established Hotevilla in the early 1900s after the tribal split at Oraibi between the then called "hostiles" and "friendlies." Hostile Hopis were the people who did not want government support, as opposed to the friendlies who did. Hotevilla's neighboring village, now known as Old Oraibi, the scene of the physical split, is reputedly the oldest settlement still in use in America.

Blue Star told me later that the three mesas are now named backwards, as Hotevilla was originally on First Mesa. After the white people settled over at Keams Canyon in about 1874, they renamed them so the mesa closest to white people would be First Mesa and so First Mesa became Third Mesa and Third first! A wonderful example of the white settlers' arrogant, egocentric nature, or was it a deliberate attempt to Heyokah (turn upside down) an area steeped in power much the same as Hitler had done by using the Hopi symbol for his own purposes, now commonly known throughout the world as the swastika. This symbol of Hopi migration will forever be seen as a generic symbol of evil. How weird is that! I remember being in the Social Security office one day in London, and I was wearing a turquoise necklace with the Hopi migration symbol on and as I was talking to the lady at the desk, she just kept staring hard at my necklace. She didn't say anything, just looked really intense. I figured she was looking to see if what she saw was actually a swastika. I doubt anyone in the Camden Social Security office was familiar with Hopi symbolism.

We picked up Blue Star from his village house and then drove down to where the Hopi Prophesy Rock was now located. I was immediately enthralled. I had never seen original rock art in anything but the British Museum. The Brits have been amazing plunderers of history and sacred artifacts from all over the world, which are now "owned" by the museum. There was nothing like seeing it in its original environment. Well, actually it had been moved from its original location to keep it safe, but the general environment was still the same. It didn't currently appear to be held in very high esteem though. It broke my heart to see the area strewn with litter and empty beer cans. How prophetic indeed that the local people were drawn to this spot to indulge in the poisons of the encroaching western world, perhaps still drawn by the unseen energy of the rock. Blue Star interpreted the hieroglyphs for us and pointed out the line on the rock that represented the Hopi path of emergence. The path the survivors of the Third World had taken out of the Ant World underground, up the corn stalk and into this world. The line then split representing the two paths the human race could take. The good path of hard work following Maasaw, planting corn and keeping the Earth sacred, or the path of greed represented by, as Blue Star called them, the Three Witches, which would eventually lead to self destruction and the end of the Fourth World, the world we currently live in.

The Hopi believe, as do their South American brothers and sisters I met in Peru, that the world has passed through three cycles since the beginning. At the end of the First, Second and Third world, human life was "purified" as it had become corrupt, greedy, and had abandoned the instructions given to it by the Great Spirit. The last cleansing was the Great Flood, which wiped out all but a faithful few. The one-hearted Hopi at that time took refuge with the Ant People underground, hence the depiction of that journey out of the Ant World on Prophecy Rock. I guess Noah, his family and the some of the animal kingdom survived on the other side of the world as well!

Blue Star turned around and walked away from where he had stood pointing out the symbols. At the same time, I turned to jump down from the rock I was standing on. Blue Star brushed past me muttering something. Ben, startled, looked up at me wide-eyed grinning.

"Did you hear what he just called you?"

"No,' I replied "what?"

"He called you a witch!" Ben replied.

"No he did not!" I exclaimed laughing, "You're having me on."

Ben started laughing even more.

"No I am not, he called you a witch!"

I turned to look at Blue Star who was now out of earshot. He stood there watching us with that implacable look on his face betraying nothing.

"Well," I said looking back at Ben grinning, "he's not far wrong is he? It's kind of a compliment where I come from. I'm not sure I want to be associated with the Witches of doom over there though." I nodded toward the pictograph. Ben grinned and Blue Star remained implacable and unmoved.

We drove the convoy back up to Hotevilla village and visited with Blue Star's family for a bit, then made our way down onto the area known now as HPL, Hopi Partition Land. The roads were much worse down on the plains of the mesa. Well, you couldn't actually call them roads, just very bumpy dirt tracks. This, of course, did not deter Ben or Will from driving as fast as they possibly could. We were meant to be meeting a guy from the Rainbow Tribe who was going to fly in and land at the mine airport in his light plane. Ben and Will were to meet him and get some aerial footage of the mine, an exhilarating prospect for the pair of them. We drove to David Oaktree's hogan where Amy, Mae and I were going to hang out and wait for them. David Oaktree lived on Big Mountain proper, as we would later call it. He was a large, thickset Indian man with a scraggly moustache who enjoyed drinking and cozying up to women whenever he got half a chance. David had one son, Ashkii, who was studying art at a nearby college, a lovely, creative lad who liked to visit, but mainly lived with his mum in Tuba City. Ash always had some really great necklaces with him he made using traditional beads. His designs had a hint of modernity, which I thought were great. Having crow medicine and not being able to let something sparkly pass me by; I had to buy some from him. They never lasted long though; the string wasn't very strong which was sad because they were really cool looking.

Oaktree's companion Tina was at home practicing making her fry bread in the kitchen. She was a beautiful, quiet, auburn-haired woman from LA who had been living on the land for some time now, herding sheep and all that. I wasn't quite sure of the reason she had found her way to the rez, but I believe it was some dysfunctional family issues and substance abuse.

After all the introductions had been made and we were settled in for the afternoon in the dark hogan, the boys drove off to their rendezvous. Amy and I did the good little wife thing and settled down to wait, cook, and drink copious amounts of coffee, smoke and talk. A few long hours later, out of the clear blue sky a snowstorm blew in, and the boys were still not back. I started pacing as the wind rattled the plastic that covered David's windows. One too many cups of strong black coffee was not helping my jitters. I was always the nervous sort, couldn't sit still very long, always needed to be active or up to something, so all the sitting around was not something I did well.

The Bennett Freeze initiated in 1974 by then Bureau of Indian Affairs director Robert Bennett, later repealed by President Obama in 2009, forbade any repairs to homes in the disputed Navajo/Hopi partition area. The freeze was issued under the pretext of the supposed land dispute between the Hopi and Navajo, and was meant to prevent the Navajo from developing the land or repairing any infrastructure. What it in fact did was far worse. David's home, like many others, was temporarily repaired with plastic sheets and anything else they could cobble together. More permanent repairs were illegal under the Freeze, as was collecting firewood, which was punishable by jail time. No one was exempt from these draconian laws, not the old, sick, or families with young children. In their defiance and desperation many a Dineh elder saw the inside of a Hopi jail for small violations like collecting firewood in winter.

As it grew dark outside, the hogan grew even darker. There was no electricity, no wood for a fire, no oil for the lamps and no running water. We all became shadow people, sitting in the cold and dark huddled with our coats on to keep warm, endlessly waiting as the wind howled and rattled against the plastic covering on the windows searching for ways to get in. I couldn't even imagine what kind of despair living constantly in those conditions could bring. It reminded me of the classic silent, black and white movie "The Wind" with Lillian Gish, where she is driven slowly mad by the incessant wind blowing.

We ate more fry bread made with cheap white flour, drank more coffee, and I smoked more cigarettes than anyone ever should. My anxiety grew with the coming storm and I started climbing the walls. Baby Mae was the only good distraction. After hours and hours of torturous waiting, imagining all sorts of foul play, we heard a vehicle approaching, bumping its way up the dirt track. Amy and I ran out to meet our returning warriors. Of course, the mission was successful and totally wild. Both Will and Ben looked like the cats that got the cream. They were so thrilled with themselves and at that moment totally encompassed the rebellious, passionate activists they were with their wild long black hair, dark skin and shining eyes. At that moment they were the most beautiful I had ever seen them. We all bundled back inside the hogan to hear their story.

At the mine airstrip, the notorious Wackenhut security had approached the plane when it landed to ask what they were doing there. (Wackenhut, now called G4S, is a private security firm with a nasty reputation for corruption within its ranks.) Will had, in a moment of pure genius, made up some story about them working for the Feds, and the security had miraculously backed off. The plane had taken off and landed safely, and the mission was accomplished successfully, much to our relief. What at first seemed like Will's brilliant blag we were to discover later carried more ominous undertones, the truth of which we would never know.

That night David took us down to his aunt's hogan where we could stay for the weekend. It was at moments like this that I truly appreciated Will. He would always help me unload the kitchen and make sure he had carried all the heavy things before he did anything else. He always made sure I was good first, unlike the white guys who would stand around watching you unload, waxing lyrical about themselves, hoping to impress. It always struck me as very strange that whenever guys want to impress you they stand around talking about themselves, cock of the walk kind of thing, and never offer to help you. Talk is cheap; putting up a shelf is more impressive. We soon made the hogan cozy along with the old cat who lived there and the puppy who we found tied up outside under the trailer. We just couldn't bear to hear him cry all night and think about him being outside in the freezing cold.

Winter's boyfriend had brought a telescope with him and set it up outside so we could see Jupiter's rings. It was an amazing sight. The sky was crystal clear and ablaze with planets and stars the likes of which you will never see in the polluted skies of the city. The clear sky meant for a cold night, and there was a smattering of snow on the ground. Whenever the fire went out during the night the temperature plummeted and made us all wake up shivering in our blankets. Will was a complete hero and kept getting up in the freezing cold to rekindle the fire as I huddled in our sleeping bag, waiting for his warm body to return.

When we woke in the morning it was a beautiful day and David's aunt arrived to see how we were doing. She showed up with some friends who had brought their hand-made jewelry for us to admire and of course buy. We shared a breakfast of eggs, bagels and strong coffee and packed up as quickly as we could. We had promised to make Thanksgiving dinner for people over at Sara Aspen's house, and there was a lot to do. Unless you lived on what was commonly known as Big Mountain Boulevard, the home sites were far apart and took time to drive to because the roads were so rough. Until you knew your way around you always had to have a local guide, it was so easy to get impossibly lost. Every dirt road looked the same and we always joked that the people the elders wanted to be found by were the only ones who would actually find them. We swore that those hogans moved in the middle of the night sometimes. You really had to get used to navigating by landmarks and not road signs. When the inclement weather came in, your landmark could get washed away and you would have to start all over again.

When we got to Sara's homestead, she commenced to scold us viciously for everything we did. We didn't cut the wood right, we didn't make the coffee right, we didn't know how to light the stove; Sara terrorized us all. Will and Ben were going to leave again on another "boys only" mission. Will laughed as I pleaded not to be left with the scary, screaming Grandma but to no avail. It was all female hands on deck in the kitchen, and there was no getting out of it. More Dineh people started to arrive, but hardly anyone spoke English. The elderly women gathered in the kitchen to drink endless rounds of coffee and watch us suspiciously like a murder of crows. I was transfixed by the energy that emanated so brightly from them and became unbearably shy. Winter got out the buffalo meat that Ben had brought with him, and we all stopped and looked at each other. I said, "Um well what the fuck do we do with that?"

I wasn't about to touch it, and no one had thought to bring a sharp knife - another thing I learned always to carry on the rez. The Grandmas watched on with their intense dark eyes, muttering to each other in Dineh. Winter finally had the presence of mind to get one of the English speaking Dineh to interpret to them that we were all vegetarians and didn't know how to cut or cook meat, so could they help us?

Apparently, that was the funniest thing they had heard for months, and it had them all cackling with laughter, which thankfully broke the ice. We made a gallon of mashed potatoes, BBQ'd corn, and meat. I think everyone enjoyed it. They thanked us very nicely anyway, and at least they all got fed.

Typically male, Will and Ben arrived just in time to enjoy the food and then off we went again back to base camp at the hogan. That night we were supposed to have a sweat lodge ceremony, but I had my "moon time," so I could not go in. On the way back Will produced some peyote medicine and offered me some. I had never taken it before so, in true indomitable Summer style, I took the spoon and swallowed two mouthfuls of the revolting tasting stuff. It was incredibly hard to get down, powder dry and the worst thing I had ever tasted. My throat revolted and threatened to close or throw everything back up. As I was trying to force it down, Will laughed uproariously and gave me some water. Gagging, I forced myself to swallow the hideous powder substance; it was the most inconceivably revolting thing I had ever tasted. Everything seemed fine until we got back to the hogan. By that time I could barely stand up, and I felt the most incredible overwhelming urge to sleep. Everyone else had taken some "medicine" but as always it didn't have the same effect on me. No, not me, I had to be special! Had to have my very own reaction to it… alone. The medicine completely and utterly wiped me out. My nose suddenly became the heaviest thing on my body and just kept heading down onto our bed. The rest of the crew circled up to share and pray and asked me to join them. Oh no, not me though, had to be the outside one. Mumbling my decline and ignoring all disapproving looks, I gave in to the great desire to lie down. It felt like I was Dorothy walking through the poppy fields in the Wizard of Oz, overcome with the Wicked

Witch of the West's sleeping spell. Cotton wool puffed out in my head and my eyelids wouldn't stay open. The fetal position suddenly felt like it was the most important thing to attain in my life. As the medicine enchanted me I curled up to snooze, I was so un-cool! Apparently that is NOT what you are "supposed" to do. You are supposed to muscle through the sleepiness and sit up and pray, or something along those lines. Well I've never been one to do what you are "supposed" to do and there was no helping it. I couldn't have stayed upright if my life depended on it.

After the others had finished their circle, Ben and the boys went up to the lodge to get the fire started. The sweat lodge was built at the Anna Mae Sundance camp, so named after Native American activist and American Indian Movement member, Anna Mae Aquash, who was found murdered on the Pine Ridge Indian reservation in 1976. For once Amy and I had the rather privileged position of not having to do any hard labor. Me, because I had my moon-time, and Amy because she had the baby. I felt some resentment from our compatriots for that, as it looked like the girlfriends of the cool dudes got out of working hard in the freezing cold, but I was past caring. Amy and I walked up to the lodge and got as close as was allowable. From there we watched the ceremony, huddled together against the night temperatures, leaning up against a low wall. I don't know how the others did it, certainly even in my best physical state wild horses would have had to drag me into that lodge. When everyone finally emerged from the lodge with soaked clothes clinging to them, the steam rolled off them in such great wafts it looked like they were bodily evaporating. It was freezing outside, but it must have felt somewhat relieving, if only for a few minutes, after the intense heat of the ceremony.

The next morning after breakfast we took off across the mountain by way of the mines. We wanted to visit some more and see the actual mine fields before going home. We stopped the convoy on the side of the road so Will could change the number plates on the jeep. Yes, highly illegal! We had switched the plates when we had first got there so that if the Hopi Rangers caught the boys they couldn't trace the car. Just as we were doing that, perhaps a tad stupidly on the side of the road, up pulled the Feds. The officer asked for everyone's drivers license except for Will's and mine. I was holding Mae at the time, so perhaps that's why he didn't ask for mine, but this was another unexplainable event that happened that weekend we were to wonder about later. Thankfully, it turned out not to be such a big hassle and he left us alone to continue on home. He didn't actually see us change the plates, or it may well have been another story. But then again, we were on the rez where laws are unto themselves, or perhaps he just thought of us as a bunch of hippies. Whatever it was, we had to wonder what on earth he was doing out there in the middle of nowhere and how come he had just happened upon us, the only cars on the road for miles. You start to learn how nothing happens by accident on the rez, and everyone is being watched. We never figured it out and nothing seemed to come of it, so it remains a mystery to this day.

When we got back to LA or Lala land as I liked to call it, Will moved in with me. He basically didn't have anywhere else to go. This was perhaps not the best of ideas, as it turned out. It would be a time of drama, nightmares, loss, grief, alcoholism and heartache for us, and it was a year before the land beckoned me again. I'm not sure that if I had listened to the warning signs about Will I would have escaped some of the pain, or as with most life lessons, it would have just visited my life in another form. I will never know, but I carry the scar on my soul to this day. Will, however, bears more scars than I. Not just from our relationship but ones that go back eons and are indelible. Who knows if those can EVER truly heal? By his account, he had been taken into a government program when very young after losing his parents and twin brother in a car accident on Pine Ridge. In yet another tragic story, his father had been driving them all whilst drunk. He was convinced he recalled being experimented on, there were always murmurings of such goings on that could never be proved. Apparently, the government was interested in tracking any potential "messiah" figure that may emerge amongst the Native Americans, so they would experiment with orphaned children from certain families to see if there were any in particular who showed special aptitude for psychic abilities. I recall one night fairly early on in the relationship, I was taking a North American Indian Archaeology class at UCLA and halfway through one class I had this overwhelming desire to go home. I couldn't concentrate on what was being said so I left early. I got home to find Will drunk, staring madly in the large living room mirror, having smashed some furniture. He was drunk and waving a switchblade around. He had that same glazed over look in his eyes, the same look that he had on our first drive up to Big Mountain together, as if he had been possessed by a darker spirit which made his eyes blacker than they where. I managed to talk him around and he slowly gave in and released the knife to me, but there were other incidents. Once, we were invited to a brunch party at a friend's house. They unfortunately thought it just fine and perhaps a little amusing to give him alcohol. After I dragged him away because of course he started to act strangely and my girlfriend was getting weirded out, we ended up at the beach where he jumped in the water and just started swimming out to sea! I thought he was going to either drown himself or just never turn around and I would have to call the lifeguard. He eventually stopped, turned around and did make it back to the beach safely. Where does a rez child from Dakota learn to swim like that? He picked up a large rock and dumped it in the back of the truck as a gift for me. I still have it sitting on the front steps! How does one cope with such odd behavior? I was totally ill equipped to deal with such a dysfunctional personality.

When we finally split up, and he walked out of the door forever, I had to go through months of acupuncture just to alleviate the garish nightmares that I had started to have every night since we had gotten together. I don't know whether I was in some way downloading memory or energy from Will, or if it was something in our past lives we had experienced together. I still keep a lock of his long beautiful black hair, the one he gave to me when he was leaving for the last time as a way of expressing the deep grief he felt.

The Return

I remember the decision to return to Big Mountain, or so I think. It was one lazy Sunday hanging out with friends; Ben suddenly turned to me and said,

"Hey, why don't you come up to the rez with me next weekend. You have a truck now, I could do with some help." Thinking back to the first journey up there and the crazy year with Will, it did not really appeal.

"Mm, no I can't," I replied, "I promised Snow Deer I would go and see her up in Ojai." Ben looked at me with those big, brown, reproachful eyes.

"You can go and see Snow Deer any time!" He was good, the guilt kicked in.

"Yes, but I promised,' I whined, "she's expecting me." Ben turned his reproachful look fully on me. That was it; I couldn't stand the scrutiny of my weak, lazy character. Now I was truly squirming. "Ok, ok, ok, I'll come." I sighed. And that was it, it was that simple: the energy from the land reached out its hooked tentacle and I was reeled in. Little did I know what was to come.

Snowdeer was a Cherokee lady who I had the greatest privilege of becoming great friends with. She was unlike any other person I have ever met and from the moment we met we became instantly bonded. Snowdeer quickly became a friend, mentor, Aunt and Soul Sister. She had a profound effect on my life. Uniquely gifted, funny, wise, magical, beautifully irreverent and deeply knowledgeable she left the planet way too early for my liking. Like so many, Snowdeer had a destructive and abusive childhood at the hands of a broken, self obsessed mother and suffered greatly. I don't know how she endured so much but she found some solace in art. Her writing was some of the most powerful, magical and truly unique stories I have ever read but she refused to have them published. She was so very afraid of being the target of abuse and I think finally when the cancer came she was ready to leave the planet. I would not be the same person I am without having met her.

III

Up on Big Mountain Christmas 1998

It was truly inspiring to be made welcome in the middle of the night on Christmas Eve by a family you have never met before. To have their children make room for strangers with sleeping bags, to feel a sense of community in a world so lacking, to share food, of which there was little. This was my second trip up to Big Mountain to deliver food and clothing donations to the resistors on the mesa. I already knew we didn't have enough food, but at least we had some, and it would help -everything helps. I had organized a food run at the animation studio I was working at and had a good response thanks mainly to my generous Irish co-workers who remembered what it was to be in need. So with that, and the donations organized by Ben and the other volunteers, we could fill our small trucks with supplies, enough at least to make a gesture of support. After the twelve-hour drive, we arrived late at the home of Greystone Pine, one of the resisting Grandmother's sons. Morgaine Stanislavski, the spokeswoman for the Sovereign Dineh Nation, was staying there temporarily. Morgaine and Greystone were to be our guides and translators on the mesa, as hardly any of the traditional elders spoke English.

Inside the house, the Christmas tree in the living room was surrounded by presents. It reminded me of home in England.

Our family tree was always burdened with many gifts, even if mum and dad didn't have much money. They always seemed to bestow on us everything we could ever want at Christmas. I can remember many a Christmas Eve arriving home hardly able to open the living room door, as there were so many presents under the tree, Mum and Dad just grinning away waiting for everyone to come home to enjoy family time. Mac, our crazy West Highland Terrier, would attack everyone that came through the door and Dad would excitedly dole out his favorite whisky, Glenfiddich or Glenmorangie, in finger width amounts, answering any problems I had with "You can always come home." It was a phrase that emboldened me as I stepped out into the world, and often wished I had before he passed but never did. This is something I regret bitterly to this day.

We laid out our sleeping bags on the floor to get a few hours rest. There was something very, very Christ-like about it all, even though I don't believe Christmas Day is the actual birth date of Jesus, it was still very meaningful and somehow sacred. We didn't actually get much sleep, as Morgaine is a Jewish girl from New York who can talk the hind legs off a donkey. One half of twins whom the Hopi elders apparently call "The Slayers" and say they are part of the Hopi Prophecy. Morgaine has incredible fortitude; a little tough to get used to but once you get to know her she is wonderful. Ben and Morgaine are as two peas in a pod, non-stop energy, quick and intelligent and they adore each other.

The next morning, bright and early, we set out across the mountain to visit as many elders as our provisions would extend to. It was crisp and cold, but the sky was a gorgeous azure blue. Snow lay on the ground in patches making the dirt roads somewhat slushy, which was always fun to drive on, even in a two-wheel drive truck. I had much fun sliding around. I should have been a rally car driver. Mum said that I used to take off so quickly in my baby wheeler and had figured out how to lift it up over the doorstep. I would be gone out the door in seconds. Seems like even as a baby I was racing to get out into the world.

It was extremely hard for me to witness so much need. With so much struggle going on in the world and with so many of our relations in desperate need of help, I find it hard sometimes to know where to put the limited extra resources and giveaways I can offer. The Dineh are a matriarchal society and so, being a woman, and as Big Mountain is so close to LA, in my back yard so to speak, I thought it was a good cause to support. I feel a great deal of respect for the elders, especially the Grandmothers of the Dineh. There are so few Grandmothers left, with such a strong bond to Mother Earth and their traditional ways, I felt it was important to help them as much as I could. And of course, I wanted to learn as much as I could about the connection they had to the Earth.

One of the things I learned was the Dineh elders say Big Mountain is the liver of Mother Earth, and I believe them. They are my Grandmothers; there is no reason to doubt what they say. I feel the Earth hurting from our greed and invasive exploitation of her resources; deep inside my guts I feel her hurting. Where once was a sacred cornfield on Big Mountain now stands a coal mine. A life sucking force ripping the blood energy from our Mother Earths liver. I understand how our society needs resources to grow and survive, but why do we always have to choose the most destructive way of going about obtaining it? There are some places that I believe must remain sacred for the future generations, so our children can live in a beautiful world and not a toxic one. Why would anyone not want that? But that is not what the dominant forces on this beautiful blue planet want right now, is it? They want to turn it into a toxic waste dump. A burnt shell of destruction where nothing beautiful survives whilst they exist in their man-made bubbles, immune to poverty, suffering, disease or pain.

During this visit, Ben took me to see the uranium dump. We stood by the barbed wire fence, just staring at a field of dangerous, contaminated yellowcake, visible to the naked eye. You can drive past the dump, or even stand right by it with the wind blowing in your face, and breath god only knows what. The dump, in turn, sits right next to the river, which flows into the Colorado and then into aqueducts that supply water to Los Angeles. The dump is surrounded by a barbed wire fence and has one sign warning of radiation hanging loosely on it. We all know how a wire fence can contain uranium, right? It's strange how seeing it makes me feel. I mean I KNOW this happens, but it's not really until you see it with your own eyes that you are stunned by the truth of how little people care. We look at each other, Ben and I, and I see my pain reflected in his eyes. It's possible that one particle could blow through our bodies as we stand there and give us cancer. The invisible death that has killed so many on this reservation. Uranium mining started on the Navajo reservation after the end of World War II. Yellowcake is a powder-like substance, which is a product of processing uranium ore. Why or how it got to this dump and just sits there I don't know, but efforts to clean up contaminated Navajo land have been sporadic and pathetic at best.

We left the dump and headed up to the Hopi mesas where we often stayed. One of my favorite moments I remember about this trip was when the daughter of a family we stayed with in Hotevilla asked if she could camp with us for the night. She asked me what Los Angeles was like; so I told her it was a huge city. She asked if it was bigger then the village. Smiling at her innocence I silently prayed that she would stay in the village and never have to make her living in a city. She in turn laughed at us trying to make a good fire in the potbelly stove, and told us we were funny. I think we are too, the strange city folk who have the ability to navigate four lanes of traffic at high speed, use computers, telephones, spas and shopping malls but can't even light a fire properly or plant corn. How far from nature have we removed ourselves? I felt more at home there than any other place I've been. Sleeping on the floor by a fire with people crashed out all around me, listening to their heavy breathing and often their snoring, like the den mother, making sure everyone was comfortable and finding comfort in hearing people drift off to sleep. There were many, many precious moments up at Big Mountain, and I'd like there to be many, many more. So for me, for as long as I'm here, I'll support the people up there who would like to keep it a special and sacred place.

IV

January 1999

For the next year or so, we organized a caravan of supplies practically every two weeks. I'm not even sure how we did that now, mainly through a lot of people's generosity. Most of the time I went, once or twice I did not. There were special missions too: meeting journalists and driving them around, introducing them to the elders, filming and documenting human rights abuses, and a variety of meetings and ceremonies. Some times we had large caravans, sometimes there were only two trucks. It was mainly Ben and I, Autumn and Winter. Lots of people came, most never came back. The weekends were always tough on the body, equally tough on the vehicles, hard work but immensely exciting and adventurous to me, the city girl from London town. There where many confrontations within our group and between supporters and the Hopi rangers. Most things were ironed out over time. Alas, the Hopi rangers continued to follow us, when they could find us! We became quite adept at avoiding them.

After one incident in particular where the rangers pulled over the food caravan and took all our license plates numbers, I decided to start practicing my 'medicine' seriously in the hope of making us invisible to the enemy. It seemed to work and continued to work. My good friend, Snowdeer, had taught me some old ways of protecting yourself psychically and energetically, kind of like building a protective psychic shield around yourself, and I would extend that to the people and vehicles traveling with us. It did seem to work but unfortunately, Winter and Autumn weren't so lucky, and whoever else were on missions alone continued to be harassed by either the rangers or the clichéd drunk, abusive Indian. Sometimes I thought that certain volunteers actually enjoyed the added drama, and then later on in life I realized that humans did enjoy and bring on drama in their life. It seemed to be a way of occupying themselves so they didn't have to look too closely at themselves, or anything else. Humans are excellent at finding distractions to keep them from living in the moment or becoming a better human.

My medicine seemed to be fairly strong, coupled with Ben's it was pretty unbeatable and our journeys up to the mountain often went without an encounter with the Hopi rangers. Our missions invariably went well if we remained attentive, sensible, clever and shielded ourselves at all times. Of course, this was always great fun for us too. Often times when we had to drive directly through Hopi country, we would sing a medicine song and maintain radio silence. It was so exciting to be on this covert adventure feeling like we were evading but at the same time counting coup (meaning touching your enemy and getting away safely), and sneaking around right under their noses. There was even a comment one day in the Hopi paper asking how white bahanas (the Hopi word for whites) from Los Angeles could manage to find the homesteads of the resisting elders, but the Hopi police couldn't! That made us all laugh. I became quite familiar with Coyote animal medicine and got great satisfaction asking for their help. In Native American lore coyote can teach you how to laugh at your own mistakes. To me they have a lot of cunning, stealth and intelligence. I always seemed to prefer and be more connected to the animals that are considered negative in some way. Negative maybe too strong a word but coyote is considered a trickster and can also act as a life lesson but with great humor. I just adore the animals that have been given a bad rap by humanity. My crow helpers, Magda and Dagda, were always around guiding me, acting as a warning signal, and being thoroughly enjoyable. The crow is another animal associated with negativity and witchcraft but to me, they are the most incredible, intelligent, beautiful birds. If there were such a thing as reincarnation, I would opt to come back as a crow.

I met many Dineh whom I became extremely fond of: Grandpa and Grandma Alder, David and Peter Oak, Tina Long (non-Dineh), Georgia and Greystone Pine, Jane, Kevin and Esther Sycamore and Sean Turtle. The dreadfully behaved yet wonderful teenagers Arthur, Percy, and Gwen. The handsome Gavin Mistletoe, the shy Blue Star, his wife Opal and daughter Sage. Incredibly, they turned out to be cousins of Keira WhiteStar, a Navajo friend of Snowdeer's I had met in Ojai who now lives in Louisiana. Sage is so special, I feel as if she helped to protect us whenever we stayed in Hotevilla, a place of great centrifugal force. Sometimes the energy there was incredibly hard to handle, sometimes it made me feel like I would die. The spirits of the world always seemed to affect me the strongest and speak the loudest when I was in Hotevilla, as if the telephone to the energies swirling around the universe were on loudspeaker there.

V

February 5th-7th 1999

One weekend in particular we had an extra large caravan going up to Big Mountain, which was very exciting for us. There was a family of Chumash from the Owl clan who brought all their kids in a huge red truck. Hawk, an ex-AIM (American Indian Movement) member, drove up with Ben and acted as security, a job he later forsook for reasons only Ben and he knew about. Winter and Autumn got along very well on this trip, only to fight continuously later on. There were Bryony and young Pete, a nice but quiet young couple from Ojai, Sun, a conservation activist and photographer from the Action Resource Center who hated us smoking but was extremely cute, and Steph, my neighbor, who had shown a lot of interest in the cause and drove with me in my small Ford truck. There were two other women whose names I forget, and Joseph Turnbull, also from AIM. Joseph later just turned out to be a complete flake; he was so full of himself. He always promised to go to AIM and discuss the issues and then return to us with a decision and some help for the elders on Big Mountain, but nothing ever materialized. Out of all the organizations that we petitioned for help, those strutting peacocks annoyed me the most. Those I met were all talk and no action as far as I could see. We took up a ton of food donations with us, including cases of macaroni, rice, beans, pasta, dog and cat food and some winter clothes.

We made it to the rez safely and all in one piece. It was slow going, lots of people to keep an eye on and stop for breaks, but it was a safe journey all round. We made base camp at Grandma Georgia Pine's homestead as usual, and rested for what was left of the night. She was by far the easiest to reach after a long journey and closest to the mine at Kayenta.

The next morning we split the caravan in two to accomplish our missions. Ben and Hawk went with Greystone and Morgaine to rendezvous with other Dineh and complete their own secret mission. Steph and I drove with the rest to deliver food. Such a large caravan could not go unnoticed on the rez, or else we had a mole, because noticed we were. Something had happened in LA when we were getting ready to leave that made me think somebody was watching us. It was one of those inexplicable moments that feel like the universe is tapping you on the shoulder to show you something, but you can't quite make out what it means. As everyone was rushing around excitedly, loading all the trucks at Ben's house, the quiet voice at the back of my mind told me to turn around and look. At that moment, a Native American guy driving a jeep drove past us, nothing too extraordinary, but something about it nagged at me. I mean, we were in a back street of North Hollywood, not exactly the place you would find an Indian guy driving past at exactly the same time we were loading up to drive to Big Mountain. Of course, I would have sounded quite paranoid by saying anything and usually when I noticed strange moments like this it was never a big deal. I made a mental note and got on with the job at hand of loading the truck and setting up our walkie talkies.

We set off across the mountain to deliver food. It was agreed that if one truck was pulled over the rest would continue in an effort to stop the whole caravan from being harassed by Hopi Rangers. Bryony and young Pete pulled up the rear guard, Sally Pine was going to act as our guide and interpreter and would ride with Autumn and Winter who were leading, and so we set off. Steph and I stayed at the back, just in front of Bryony and young Pete. On our way down Big Mountain Boulevard, the main dirt road that ran from Rocky Ridge over to the coal mine, Bryony and Pete were pulled over by the Hopi rangers. I guess we really were too big to miss. That left Steph and I in the rear, so I slowed down and then stopped at a safe distance to watch what was happening. I knew it wasn't quite what we had agreed but as a veteran of the food runs it seemed rude to leave the new volunteers alone to deal with the rangers, especially as I had a better idea of where we were going and, if we lost the main caravan, could guide us all. The rangers seemed like they were making a big deal out of things, and I started feeling really uncomfortable abandoning them. Steph and I decided to turn around and go help, but just as I was maneuvering the truck, we saw Pete and Bryony get back in the truck and pull away. We continued on to catch up with the rest of the caravan, but unfortunately, that wasn't the end of the surprise. At the junction of the 140 to Coal Mine Mesa, the rest of a Hopi showdown was waiting for us, and as we drove up, we saw the rangers had detained the entire caravan. I guess at that point we should have continued driving, but there was nothing for it; it was obvious we were all together. It was a good job Morgaine and Hawk weren't with us, as that was more than likely whom they were looking for.

As we pulled up, Winter stalked over to my truck window and started jabbing her finger in my face. She was really mad at Steph and I for stopping and breaking "the rule." I tried to tell her we felt bad for leaving Bryony and Pete and really we had stopped far enough away not to be involved, but she wouldn't listen. She just kept jabbing her finger at me and screaming until I finally just got annoyed and started rolling up the window saying over and over again, "Just step away from the truck, step away from the truck." Steph was laughing and being incredulous at the same time. I felt the small altercation was badly timed on Winter's part; there was no need to show dissent in the ranks in front of the rangers. Winter didn't have any authority over my decisions, and I was quite capable of looking after Steph and myself. As the rangers started to take down everyone's license plate number, one of them came over to talk to us. Steph and I decided to act like a couple of dumb blonde Californians. We rolled down the window and I leaned over eyeing him admiringly saying,

"Are you a real Indian? I've never met one before!" The young ranger succumbed to our brilliant acting, or maybe we just didn't have to act too much, and he suddenly became bashful replying,

"Sure ladies, I'm a real Indian." We both gasped in amazement and continued to chatter at him aimlessly. He eventually put away his notebook without having written down a single thing and smiling broadly at us waved us a fond goodbye. Sometimes just being nice really works. Steph and I laughed uproariously as we watched Winter continue to fume and stalk around yelling at the Hopis who were writing down her license plate number.

At the time, it frustrated me to see that the majority of the white Americans I was with, in my opinion, were taking themselves way too seriously. Even though the Hopi rangers were in essence harassing us, we ourselves had made the mistake of looking like a caravan and being very obvious. We learned a great lesson here though, for future caravans we would not all drive so closely together, and would stay in contact via walkie-talkies instead. Needless to say, when we had rendezvoused with Morgaine later on, the subject of whether to confront the Hopi rangers or have a more Zen approach was raised by Winter, who was needing to be validated, and the camp remained divided. There were those who preferred the "wily coyote" approach of extracting ourselves from encounters by any means possible, and those who wanted a full-on confrontation all of the time. Winter thought that any time the Hopi rangers stopped us constituted an infringement of our civil rights and an attempt to stop us helping the Dineh, and should be battled over.

Choose your fights, that is what I say and a running battle with the Hopi rangers is a dud as far as I am concerned. My energies were best saved for the real struggles to come. The fewer enemies we had searching for us the better. I do hate being told how to cook my eggs though. On this trip, it felt like I had micromanagers and control freaks surrounding me. Oh my god! If the eggs didn't get cooked the way Winter wanted them cooked, you would think the whole world would fall apart. So I continued defiantly to cook them in my own way and told her to back off brandishing my wooden spoon. My mum always said I hated being told what to do, and to make matters worse; I seemed to have landed in country where everyone excels at telling other people what to do!

As night dropped down its inevitable curtain and the world went to sleep, us wolves slept in Grandma Pine's hogan guarded by Hawk lying stretched across the door. I slept too close to the fire, and, forgetting that coal gets incredibly hot, nearly set myself alight. Like Icarus flying too close to the sun, I fly too close to my sun and risk getting burned in more ways than one.

The heat from the stove glowed on my cheeks and I laughed at myself, waking up sweating, bundled too heavily in blankets and clothes. We had been freezing up here before and now I was wearing too much, but there were too many men around to disrobe, so I continued to sweat. Hawk noticed I had woken up, laughed and said, "Don't worry I would have put you out." I lay awake for a while, listening to the racket all the snoring bears in the hogan were making and feeling alive.

VI

Gathering Of Nations

It was the weekend of the 'Gathering of Nations' benefit that Ben was organizing. I was lucky; it turned out that the elders stayed with me. Kevin, Esther and Jane Sycamore and Georgia Pine. David Oak, the kids and some others stayed with a lady called Rachel in Sun Valley. Although I was quite unprepared, having more to do with the fact I had forgotten how much food that many people could consume, it was a great weekend. The main point is that two very important meetings took place at my house, and I felt quite honored to have that opportunity. Ben laughingly called it the 'Summer's Summit.'

I called Esther and Jane Sycamore the "Purple Grandmas," as they always seem to both wear shades of purple, which is quite a magical color. They were also two of my favorite elders. Very kindly ladies whose wrinkled faces always shone with good humor and love, with all that they go through it's amazing they still emanate such radiance. This trip they gave me a handmade pinon nut necklace as a way of thanks, which I cherish to this day. I remember laughing as they explained to me in halting English how everything looked the same to them in LA, so they recognized my house by the seeds that lay scattered on the path fallen from the tree outside the door. The same thing I think about the rez, which they easily navigate, but without a road sign I'm lost! I watched Esther weaving once; it was so hypnotic I could have fallen into a deep slumber right there. I have one of her beautiful weavings hanging on my wall to this day. I wish I had more.

The elders were meeting with a new attorney called Charles Miller. Morgaine had discovered him somewhere along the line, and we had great hopes for good things to start to happen. The new attorney specialized in environmental cases, so we would focus on the environmental devastation and the human rights violations occurring up on the mountain. Even now it is so hard for me to put into words what happened that weekend. During the actual meeting between twenty to thirty people were sitting in my house. I didn't realize it could hold that many! All the elders who had traveled down from the mountain were there, as was Morgaine Stanislavski, Greystone Pine, Charles Miller the attorney from New York, Kim and her boyfriend from the now defunct Action Resource Center, Autumn, Winter, Sean Turtle, David Oak, the lovely Gavin Mistletoe (all Dineh), the terrible teenagers Arthur and Perce, and Gwen; Tracey, a Native American screenwriter, David (another screenwriter who was caught recording the meeting, which shocked us all) and Sidney, a homeless Dineh whom Winter had picked up on Venice Beach. That's another story entirely. No one knows this, but I had seen Sydney in Venice, drunk and in a terrible state a few weeks earlier, he had caught my eye for some reason. Ben just happened to talk to him on another weekend, and then Winter went to retrieve him and brought him along! Amy and Mae were there giving me much needed support on the hostess front. It was just people, loads of people everywhere. That weekend was such a drain I couldn't get off the couch for days afterwards, and I couldn't stop crying. Of course, what was actually discussed at that meeting was private and no one apart from Charles was allowed to take notes, so I have forgotten for the most part what was discussed. It's regrettable now, but we were so afraid of infiltration. In hindsight someone from Gaia Communications should have been taking notes as well to ensure there was a copy. It was early days on the computer front. I had prided myself on buying one of the first Apple laptops; it would feel like a cumbersome machine now but back then it was state of the art. I wish I had more insight as to how the Internet and computers would take off. I wish I had more insight in everything really. Eventually, Charles, the attorney who had called the meeting went the same way as all the other attorneys who had supposedly come to 'help' the Dineh. Who knows what really happened to those guys. Do they suddenly realize they cannot win this struggle, or does someone get to them?

VII

Gaia Communications Run March 5th 1999

The caravan consisted of five vehicles; four SUV's, one car and one U-Haul trailer. We were carrying approx. 4000lbs of dog food, of which there were still 50lbs remaining in LA because we didn't have the space to haul it, 1000lbs people food, four disposable cameras, 7000lbs of blue corn seeds, pinto bean seed, squash seed, zucchini seed (not quite a ton!). Crayons and coloring books, lamp oil, four boxes of assorted clothes, two bags, one lamp, and various personal items requested by certain elders.

With us on this trip were representatives from various Los Angeles based organizations; Sun and Ann from Action Resource Center, Steven from the Harmony Keepers, Winter from Food Not Bombs and Gaia Communications, Joseph Turnbull from AIM, Tim from San Cayentano circle, and Ben, Alice, Autumn and myself from Gaia Communications. Support for this caravan also came from Unity of Nations and No Nukes. The food was kindly donated by the Christian Church. Valuable information and support came from Black Mesa Indigenous Support Group. We were also in contact with a group called the Iron Circle Nation, from San Pedro CA, and were using this trip to fulfill a request, the details of which have been lost to time.

Tim and Joseph left LA together and went down to San Diego where 125 boxes of food were waiting to be picked up. They continued on to Big Mountain via Phoenix, but about twenty miles outside of Phoenix their truck engine caught fire. They had just fueled up and were back on the road when the motor cut out. They pulled off the road as soon as they could, and discovered the engine was on fire but had not seen any smoke. They had to use water to put the fire out because the earth was too hard packed to dig up sand. It turned out it wasn't a gasoline fire; it was electrical, and that in turn had ignited insulation that had fallen down from the hood. The final analysis: a rat had made a nest in the insulation! They limped on into Phoenix, replaced the burned wires and made repairs. They eventually stopped close to Big Mountain at 3:30am, caught a couple of hours' sleep by some railroad tracks, and then drove the rest of the way to meet us at Grandma Pine's. What an adventure they already had before they even got to the mountain!

Autumn and Winter arrived just before dawn and made coffee for everyone. Meanwhile, Alice and Ann met up with Morgaine Stanislavski and Greystone Pine who were waiting at a nearby gas station for a major news network to arrive from Colorado.

Ben and I left LA around 5:30pm in his jeep. Just two hours earlier Ben had received a phone call that his dear friend, Terence Unity Frietas, and two other human rights activists we did not know personally, Ingrid Washinawatok and Lahe'na'e Gay, were all slain execution style while on a humanitarian mission in Colombia. Terry was a Los Angeles based environmental activist who had become involved with the U'wa people of Colombia's fight against the Occidental Oil companies drilling on their land. This of course tormented Ben and made for a very sad journey. It seemed we were at the pinnacle of environmental activists being targeted for their work. It had become a dangerous business in which to care, and this assassination shocked our community and really hit our hearts hard.

It was a long, very slow drive hauling the trailer full of dog food and other donations. It gets toughest in the early hours of the morning, when your eyes are blurring the lights of the cars, and the road is dark. I only drove for a while, and Ben and I would take turns sleeping in the back of the jeep. We had to drive slowly because of the weight of the trailer. It's a good feeling to get on the mesa, but a strange ominous silence always fills the truck as you drive past the mine where once was a sacred cornfield. A light snow had sprinkled the ground, which made it stressful to drive with the constant worry of black ice. It was such a sad trip as the memory of a murdered spiritual warrior, a fallen angel, filled my friend's mind. I did not know Terry, yet I felt the loss of a fellow guardian of the Earth very deeply.

We arrived at Grandma Georgia Pine's house at 9:30 am the next morning. We took the time for our first cup of coffee with Grandma while her daughter Sally translated to her mother the news about Terry's execution. About a year and a half earlier, Georgia and six other Dineh elders had met Terry and a spokesperson for the U'wa tribe at a prophecy conference in Sedona. Georgia said she remembered her meeting with Terry in great detail. After that meeting the U'wa representative Roberto, Terry, and Ben traveled back to LA together. Soon after in Columbia, Roberto was thrown off a cliff and barely survived. He had been abducted and brutalized and left for dead for his work opposing oil drilling on the U'wa ancestral grounds. The U'wa have a very similar belief system to the Dineh, which connects them. The U'wa consider oil to be the blood of Mother Earth, the extraction of oil would be extremely destructive not only to their physical world but also their spiritual world. Just as the Dineh consider coal the liver of the Earth; oil is considered the blood that runs through the veins. If you think of the rainforest as the lungs of the Earth, then she does start to look alive, doesn't she? Two major oil companies are responsible for the oil drilling on U'wa land: U.S based Occidental, whose headquarters are in LA, and multi-national Royal Dutch Shell. It was hotly rumored that the oil companies had paid the guerrilla group FARC to kill Terry and his companions. This was the first time in my life it really started coming home to me how far these corporations would go to protect their interests, and their obscene need to expand their wealth. People and the planet were collateral damage that meant nothing. Where do they think they're going to live once they have destroyed the planets eco-system?

As we drank our coffee, lamenting the loss of our warrior friend, Winter coordinated the teams for the food drop. We decided to begin delivering food to the families closest to the mine whilst we waited for Morgaine, Greystone, and the others. First, we gave Georgia her supplies, which helped to lighten the load. We left her thirteen cases of dog food, five boxes of human food, a twelve-pack of toilet paper, one case of mixed food grain bars, chicken broth, and lamp oil. Georgia's family requested a basketball for the kids, solar panels and a generator, cleaning supplies: mops, dish soap, etc., garden tools: rake, hoe etc. squash, pumpkin, cucumber, watermelon and cantaloupe seeds, white rice, cornmeal, peanut butter, and pinto beans. Grandma specifically explained to us that they get a lot of donations of kidney beans but don't eat them; the Dineh like pinto beans. Georgia's granddaughter needed a backpack, pens and pencils for school. All of these requests we listed in the hopes of getting some donations back in LA. I didn't like to make promises but if we had specific requests then sometimes we could find people willing to donate those items, and I always loved delivering them when we'd been successful.

First we visited Grandma Mae Pine's Hogan, as she didn't live too far from Georgia's. She wasn't home, so we left five boxes of food and five cases of dog food outside her door. It always made me happy to leave gifts for people who are not home. Hopefully, it is a nice surprise for them once they get back home.

The caravan slowly moved off, heading towards Big Mountain Blvd to visit the families there. We started to pick up some unknown radio sources speaking Dineh on the walkie-talkies. We were probably being followed but couldn't tell for sure. Ben accidentally took the wrong road, but as it turns out a mysterious man, whom we thought was spying on us, followed us down the wrong road, so we had our proof we were being followed. He was driving a red and white bronco and had a good look at us whilst pretending to mind some sheep. The trouble was the sheep kept running away from him, a sure sign they don't know who the hell you are!

Next stop was Betty Rivers' house, but we couldn't easily get to it. The Hopi rangers had bulldozed her driveway, piling dirt up to stop anyone in a vehicle getting to her hogan. This is another ploy they use to harass the Grandmas to move and to stop any supporters from driving up with supplies. Well, that wasn't about to stop us, so the boys hefted the heavy sacks on their shoulders and hiked the food in anyway. They make you so proud when you see men in their element helping people and doing the work. Our mystery friend in the white cap tried to blend in with the sheep in the meadow opposite, but the sheep dogs where giving him away by barking furiously, which made us all laugh uproariously. I can hardly believe the lengths the Hopi rangers will go to stop an elderly woman, who was born and has lived in the same place her entire life, from getting any help or being able to drive up her own driveway in a truck to carry supplies in. It's pure evil.

Prairie Meadow and Rachel Vail, who lived together, were next on the route. Through us, they requested some sky blue paint and two women supporters to help them paint their house. I loved the idea of a sky blue hogan; it seemed so outrageous and creative. The traditional Navajo women are very particular about certain things, mixing with the opposite sex is one of them. It would appear inappropriate and also uncomfortable for them to deal with strange men in their home without a man around themselves. The Grandmothers who live alone prefer the company of female supporters unless, of course, they are in a relationship or married. It's extraordinary how often you heard tell of people behaving in a totally inappropriate manner like wearing skimpy clothes and propositioning the men. Even the old men! Grandma's Meadow and Vail were very specific about having female help, as they felt very strongly it would be inappropriate to have men staying with them alone. Also, the hogans usually only have one room, and everyone has to sleep in the same room, so I could understand them wanting female help.

The Dineh have a definite etiquette when it comes to relationships and dress codes. The women supporters must wear clothes that aren't see through and cover their shoulders and knees. It's also considered inappropriate for men to have their shirts off when women are around. Even now this has rubbed off on me, and I dislike seeing men not wearing shirts in public unless it's by the beach or pool. The Dineh are also meticulous about hygiene and some of the hippy supporters find themselves in the strange position of actually not being clean enough for the Dineh! You really do have to be quite hygienic when you live so close to the Earth. Actions like washing your hands before you sit to eat, even if there is no running water, are a part of their daily ritual. Every hogan always has a basin of soap and water near the entrance for people who come in to eat so they can wash their hands first. I have had to tell many supporters about this, and it's amazing how many folks feel uncomfortable doing this. We are so used to having instant running water, and the simple act of washing your hands in front of other people seems to cause great discomfort to some white people. Even saying hello to everyone in the room when you walk into someone's house seems to be uncomfortable for some. I mean you wouldn't walk into a white persons house and ignore half the room would you? They why on earth do that to the Dineh? It's appropriate etiquette on the rez to introduce yourself to each person in the room and lightly shake their hand. This again goes against the custom of firm handshakes that, in our western society, predominantly signifies you are a strong person. For the Dineh, gripping someone's hand hard is akin to trying to steal their energy. Next on the list was Missy who was also not home, so we left five cases of food and a few cans of carnation milk, which was always a treat on the rez to put in coffee.

We went back to Georgia's house to pick up Morgaine and Greystone, who had returned from waiting at the nearest gas station for CBS. They had waited three hours for their contact and then decided to give up. Most media do not realize what it takes just to meet them somewhere. When they don't show up it's a big blow and costs us precious time and money. Gas is very hard to come by, and not many Dineh have the means to earn the money to pay for it. We were so lucky to have Greystone Pine's support. He works at the mine but also actively participates in the Dineh resistance, which works against the mines. Without his help, we would be so much worse off. He donates so much time and money for his people's fight and drove Morgaine around in their tireless efforts to win a reprieve to the relocation. We ate some lunch at Georgia's for much needed energy. We had been running on our regular diet of coffee, bagels and cigarettes.

The afternoon of the first day on the rez is about the time the lack of sleep really kicks in and your body tries to make you lie down, so it's good to eat something to pick up some energy and continue on. It's a shame the diet is so meat based up on the mountain. When the first white supporters started arriving, many of them were environmental activists who were vegans or vegetarians. Luckily, I wasn't the first, so the Dineh were fairly used to it by the time I came along and politely refused to eat the mutton stew. On the odd occasion, I came across someone who would get offended when I declined to eat meat, but funnily enough it was always men, and I found it more about ego than anything else. The Grandmas always just laughed at our differences and found them amusing and strange. Not the least thing they found strange was the way we allow our cats and dogs to live in the house, quite the opposite to the Navajo whose domesticated animals live outside. Just like everywhere though, there were some exceptions to this rule, like Ruby Willow, who was so attached to her animals there were often kittens or baby animals penned up close to the stove for warmth. Much to my chagrin though, being born Native American doesn't instantly make you a good animal caretaker.

There were always plenty of kids around of all ages, from babies to teens, and they took a big interest in our arrival. I always felt so bad for them, especially the teenagers who didn't have much. It's so tough to be that age anyway; I wonder how they cope with the inevitable boredom that comes with being a teenager, along with the destruction of their culture and lifestyle with nothing to replace it. They didn't seem as if they do much, just hang around outside even when it's freezing! Some of the families share a one-room house with all of their children. If they're lucky they will get a small trailer for the older ones to live in so they can have some privacy and discuss the usual teen topics: the latest music and whom they like. Drugs are a problem, and even though they have no money they seem to be able to occasionally score weed. God knows where they get it from and how they pay for it. I guess its better then huffing glue, which I'm sure, is a problem as well, as is the usual alcohol addiction. Mind you that's not just a problem with the teens. Such poverty, such despair, such struggle make drugs and alcohol a cheap distraction to numb the mind and provide a few hours away from their harsh world. In the stone cold sober light of day, choosing to get stoned or drunk above buying food seems like a wasted choice, but the depression takes over and any relief from that by sinking into imagination and fantasy sounds like a welcome reprieve, albeit a brief one. That coupled with hundreds of years of brutal oppression is a fatal brew. I can't even imagine how the elders turn out to be as light and as beautiful as they are. They are like looking at a rich tapestry, woven with wisdom and ancient knowledge.

Grandma Georgia was very hospitable, as are all Navajo and Hopi people. We usually stayed in her large hogan which is wonderfully warm and cozy, not to mention the good vibes from all the ceremonies that have taken place in there. That night though there was an all-night ceremony going on, so we stayed in the kids' room of Grandmas house, all bundled up together against the cold. The kids' room was an eclectic mix of bunk beds, stored food and other goods.

The next day a blaze of phone calls occurred between Gaia Communications and other groups around the country about Terry's murder. Ben was also trying hard to stay in contact with the co producer and editors of the Geneva video via cell phone, which often doesn't work on the mountain. The Geneva video is about a recent trip the elders made to appeal to the UN. It was being edited the entire time this caravan was on the mountain and decisions needed to be made about last minute adjustments to the script. The editors worked frantically for completion by Tuesday so that it could be made available for a meeting with a major potential contributor to the legal funds of the Sovereign Dineh Nation (SDN).

The mornings always seemed to pass by too quickly, it took a long time to get everything accomplished, and a long time to get everyone motivated to leave. Grandma Georgia's homestead overlooked the mine, and as I stood outside waiting, the poetic tragedy of the place filled me with awe. Where once were sunny cornfields now stood huge foreboding machinery and dark excavations into the liver of the Earth. The coalmine has obliterated all signs of any cornfields. The crows flew overhead as if hearing my forlorn thoughts. I remember one time Ben and I stopped to plant blue corn around the mine, praying it would somehow magically act like Jack and the Beanstalk and impede the mine's progress. To cheer myself up I decided to test out the dog food we brought with us. The dogs loved it, so did the cats and even the chickens had a peck at it. One of my favorite things to do is to feed all the animals. They're all half starved all the time, much like the people.

After lunch, the caravan divided into two to cover more territory. Team 1 consisted of team leaders Greystone Pine and Morgaine Stanislavski, with Ben and Joseph Turnbull on security detail. I acted as documentation specialist (journal and video), and Sun Do did what he does best: take photographs. Tim Wilcox, agricultural specialist, and Ann, who was a professional Crisis Assessment Manager were also riding with us.

Team 2 consisted of point person and security Peter Ash, Winter on video, Autumn documenting everything, Alice, the rookie, on observation, and Steven from the group "Harmony Keepers" on security.

Team 1 set off across the mesa to deliver the supplies. We first visited Grandpa Ken and Grandma Abby Acorn. Both of these elders had serious coughs. They asked us for winter squash, corn, cantaloupe and watermelon seeds. They also requested chickens, chicken wire and roosters.

As we were doing our rounds Ben received a phone call from Keira Harvey, who lived in New York. She was very upset about Terry's death and expressed her compassion to us for the families of our slain activist brothers and sisters. Keira, a woman of great integrity, had been selling the Grandmothers' handmade rugs for the past two months in New York, and via the Internet at a time when the Internet was still in its infancy. The wool for the rugs came mainly from the Dineh's own sheep, supplemented sometimes by store bought wool for extra color when they couldn't get the natural dye. Keira had supported all of the New York based United Nations trips the elders had made of late; she also worked hard to raise funds for the Geneva trip

Onwards across the mountain.

When we arrived at Eve Singer's homestead, we decided not to drop any food there, as she was not in and three builders from the Navajo Tribal Council were on her property. Unfortunately, we just couldn't trust they wouldn't take the supplies for themselves, so we didn't leave anything.

Next stop for Team 1 was a meeting at White Bear's and first on the agenda was a discussion on Geneva. While waiting for Ben to talk with White Bear, Ann fed their dogs and a cute puppy. All the families have dogs that are all skinny, flea bitten, weepy-eyed mongrels, but are nonetheless very friendly. We all feel for them and would like to get some more help with donations for the animals. Winter had recently been working on securing more dog food and getting veterinarian help, which I hoped would come through.

While the others were in the meeting, Joseph Turnbull wrote the following entry for our journals.

"I was told once that these people live to walk in beauty, they live in that beauty, and all day today I have walked in sight of that beauty. For the first time I have some understanding of what they mean, they need to be left alone to live on their sovereign land. Peabody wants to scar the face of that beauty and the face of life itself. What that means for these people is genocide. We need to get to the heart of the issue instead of just putting out fires. This work is good, it shows a good heart and it does good things, but it does not accomplish the whole of the job. We have to get this information out to the world, so that they can know the crimes that are happening on this sovereign land. This is the war we fight."

Dramatic and beautiful words from someone I never saw on the land again!

Once the meeting was over we drove on to Coyote and Corn Lady who were building a Hogan. Of course, they were not "allowed" to build a hogan because of the Bennett Freeze, so locations and names had to remain top secret. We left them supplies and then moved onwards to Sara Aspen's homestead. We gave Sara three boxes of groceries and three boxes of dog food. She told us she needed dish soap and laundry soap, which should be fairly easy to procure for her on the next visit. Two weeks earlier, Grandma Sara had trouble with her truck, so Ben and Hawk drove to Tuba City, which is at least a 150 mile round trip, to get her a battery for the truck. They proceeded to become the saviors of the day by producing the finest battery you ever did see, connecting it, fixing the fuel line and getting the beat-up old truck going. Before Ben and Hawk had offered to go and get the battery, Grandma Sara was going to walk to Tuba City to get the battery and carry it in a backpack all the way home. Would you let anyone do this, let alone your Grandmother? These elders are so incredibly stoic. Sun's comment for our journal on the Big Mountain situation was "It sucks."

We visited Harry Black and his family, who had lots of children. We had never been to his homestead before. The dilapidated hogan was set far back on the plains of the mesa against some craggy bluffs. Harry Black and his family received seven boxes of groceries and five cases of dog food.

The sun began to set as we drove away from Grandpa Black's house. The sunsets on Big Mountain are so awe-inspiring, as you get a full 180-degree view of it. This time, the clouds turned purple and looked like fire. You could see the San Francisco Peaks.

I asked the people in our car what the clouds reminded them of. In her beautiful French accent Ann said, "A little blanket." Both Ben and Sun said, "Terry." Then amazingly the clouds turned into two huge blue eyes, watching us from above. Ann delighted us all by singing some French songs and we watched as the first evening star appeared in the glorious heavens.

Next stop, my favorites: Grandma and Grandpa Alder and their granddaughter. We arrived at their homestead about 6:30 pm and delivered about four cases of groceries and four cases of dog food. The last time we were there, Grandma and her granddaughter were weaving baskets. At ten years old, Rose was already very good at weaving. She also made a killer fry bread. How many ten year olds do you know that can weave a basket and whip up some fry bread for a group of people who turn up unexpectedly? We have lost the art of showing our kids how to take care of themselves and others. When I first met Grandma and Grandpa Alder, and shook hands with Grandpa Alder, he said,

"Your hands are cold. You must be from the North."

"Indeed I am," I replied, "that would be true." Not only is England on the same equatorial line as Canada, ergo "north" of Arizona, on the medicine wheel I "sit" in the North. I had learned from a very dear Cherokee friend a little about the Native American medicine wheel, and how people's characteristics determine which cardinal direction they are more likely to be inclined to.

Once, when I was traveling in Peru on a spiritual adventure visiting the sacred sights, I became deathly ill from some cut fruit I had eaten. After I had recovered somewhat we traveled up to Lake Titicaca, one of the highest and most sacred lakes in the world and a place I had always dreamed of going after seeing a photograph of it in a magazine. It was one of those images I get enchanted with and my obsession doesn't end until I've been. It is said that Lake Titicaca is a place where the original people emerged at the very beginnings of the human race and it is a place where many strange stories abound. We had the most amazing hotel room overlooking the lake, and on a night where the full moon shone brightly, hovering over the lake, I woke up from a very powerful dream about people from the North's frozen grounds. I love the North where snow blankets the ground; so pure, so powerful. I hate being cold, mind you, but there is something about the North that is very attractive to my soul. I dreamed of being with someone who was holding me in this arctic north place. A polar bear and a wolf were coming towards me. The person I was with indicated that I should touch the animal, but as they were wild I was scared and yet captivated. I reached out to touch them and oh, I was filled with such great joy and recognition. They were so soft and wonderful to touch and tears welled up in my eyes. Faces seem to appear through the animal faces and it felt like they were shapeshifters of sorts. I was very happy to connect with them again; it felt good although I have no idea why or how I knew them. The place dissolved and I found myself standing in a building with lots of men and women. The events that followed are not quite clear. All the people were dancing and I wanted to dance. A girl came up to me and took my purple rucksack from me saying,

"Let me carry this for you while you are here so you can be free of your burden." As she put it on she fell on her butt straight away and kinda said,

"Phew! Your ancestors are heavy!" I knew it was heavy and held out my hand to help her up but it was ok and actually quite funny.

As I started to dance I felt very sexual with these people. There was a man with a painted face dancing near me; his face appeared close to mine. I don't remember the pattern; only that it was kind of brownish and round. As we danced I broke my thumbnail, which hurt very much. The girls told me to let the painted man suck my thumb, and it would feel better, so I did. It was the strangest most erotic feeling I ever did have, the energy from the man was exquisite so I closed my eyes. When I opened them again, the people were arranging where to go later. We had moved to the stairs, and as the painted man lifted me up and twirled me around, I received a huge shot of erotic electricity right through me. He put me down and said that I should meet him at his house. The girls around me kind of giggled and oohed and aahed at us. He left to go outside and when he returned his face was clean. He sat down by the window. It was then that I noticed outside the window and was captivated by the view. In the distance was a lake surrounded by giant sculptures. Just under the surface of the lake were lights making patterns in the shape of animals, perhaps a deer, I forget now. Then it turned into a Kachina (a Hopi ancestral spirit) and then another animal. At the same time, the painted man who now had a clean face was smiling at me and asking if I had ever seen that kind of lake before. I said no I hadn't, and felt a sense of truth inside me. He was smiling and told me the lake's name, which unfortunately I didn't quite hear clearly. One of the women, and I want to call them "sprites," as these people were so light and airy, musical and dancing, was pulling my silver and turquoise ring off my finger. At the same time, I turned to the man and asked,

"Why is she taking my ring?" I was also worried that he found me rude for not listening to him, but my impression was that it was fine as the name of the lake was so secret, and he knew I would write it down, so it was ok for me not to remember it anyway. He smiled and said,

"Come with blue, go with gold, what is most precious is inside of you," and somehow indicated to my solar plexus without pointing. I felt gold glow inside the sprite woman that took my ring and as I turned back to the man, because more than anything I wanted to be with him, a door banged and I woke up to my companion saying,

"Love, do you want to see the moon?" I couldn't speak, I was so disappointed to be awake, but I heard the man say,

"It's ok, look at the moon, look at the shining path reflected in the lake and think of us."

So I turned over to look out of the window, the moon was up again in a crescent, and there was the most beautiful silvery path of the moon reflected in the water. It was the most powerful vision dream I remember ever having and it left me feeling very good.

Grandpa Alder told us that the BIA showed up at the house the prior week and twisted the arm of a young white supporter, trying to intimidate her to leave. They took pictures of this, but like much else I doubted anything could be done about it. The BIA seemed to have free range to do anything they wanted, including physical harassment. The Alder's house was in very bad repair, again due to the Bennett Freeze. The ceiling's fiberglass insulation was falling down, and we were very concerned for Grandma, who'd had a persistent cough for a while. Tom thought that as the insulation had mold on it, the spores might be contributing to her bad health. Even worse than that, after discussing trying to get help to repair the house, Ben informed us that Grandpa might have built the house from uranium tailings before he knew what it meant. Grandpa had picked up the building material from the uranium mine he had worked at years ago. Of course, they had not been informed that the material was dangerous and were not given any protection at all. We needed to get a Geiger counter out there as soon as possible to determine if the house was hot. It is very hard to imagine how bad it must feel to think you have built your own family house out of deadly material. It was a pitiful situation made even more pitiful by the lack of light. The elders mainly used gas lamps, which bathed the house in an eerie light and made the disrepair look like some ghastly Victorian nightmare.

A year earlier, Ben took a trip up to the mountain with a Geiger counter to document radiation contamination. Half a mile outside of the small town of Cameron, a hundred yards from the road, next to a trading post, he documented uranium radiation readings of 1600 rads a minute. This area was completely accessible to children and was surrounded by pools of water that were stained yellow from yellow cake. At another site, one hundred yards from the elementary school in Cove, Arizona, he documented 800 rads a minute. He recorded both of these events on videotape, dangerously exposing himself to the radiation. Nothing was ever done to clean up these sites. No surveys to see if the cancer rate was higher in these areas, no one cared. The racism against Native Americans was shocking to me. I had no idea they were still treated as badly as you see in the silly Hollywood films. Native Americans, the national sacrifice.

After visiting the Alders, Morgaine joined James, Ben and I in the Gaia Communications jeep and we drove to visit with Grandma Eucalyptus, who lives in a dugout in the side of the mountain. The dugout was actually inside the Earth herself, and was the most incredible place, overlooking a deep, rugged canyon of outstanding beauty and awe-inspiring grandeur. The coal there was easy to see, it ran across the mesa as strata of black, close to the surface. In certain places if you kick at the dirt you will find black dust just under the surface. In the deep canyons, you can see many varying shades of reds, oranges, browns and black that stripe the walls. It's a geological heaven and I often wish I had been intelligent enough to take up a career as an archaeologist or geologist. We arrived at the dugout well after dark and unfortunately, Grandma was not home. We left eight boxes of groceries and four boxes of dog food. The last time we were there, our hearts broke as we discovered that just hours earlier Grandmother and her family had to butcher her mule for food. Perhaps if we had not slept after the fifteen hours of driving we would have arrived in time to deliver food, and she would not have had to butcher the poor creature. She needed the mule to get down into the canyon to her cornfield, and because of her remoteness she did not know we were coming. When I walked into the supply hut to drop off the boxes, the bloody mule's head was sitting on the ground. It was an absolute nightmare for me, like something out of Lord of the Flies, and I couldn't go back inside. I had felt so appalled and upset that I emptied my truck and left her everything of any use I had, including my own blankets. In later visits it would always make me smile to see my pink, checked blanket sitting on her bed. That was a darn good blanket purchased from the store in Ojai and I couldn't bear the thought of it not being used. Funny how things like having a good blanket become important to you when survival and not luxuries are the most important thing. I never did find a good enough replacement until my friend Snowdeer gifted me with a medicine blanket she had, but that was too precious to use for camping in the rough.

It was no mean feat to get out of that canyon in the dark. There were a few dirt roads that crisscrossed each other, and one wrong turn in the dark could get you lost or stuck for hours. Everything looks exactly the same, and even though the ground looks solid it isn't and you can sink in the sand easily. There was also an incredibly steep hill to climb, luckily not very long, but extremely treacherous in the bad weather. If you fell over the edge, you would plunge hundreds of feet into the canyon. The Grandmas always got extremely anxious with us if we lingered and they felt a storm threatening. It was always best to travel with two vehicles, that way if anything happened to one truck you had another that could either pull you out or go for help. Before we left the canyon, we delivered eight boxes of groceries and two cases of dog food to Ruby Willow. We also delivered six boxes of groceries and four boxes of dog food to Black Wolf.

After all the deliveries, it was getting late, around 9pm, and we were getting tired, or should I say exhausted. Tired was a given on these missions as we traveled all day delivering food, maybe staying for some coffee and chatting, especially with Grandpa and Grandma Alder. We had some trouble with the vehicles. Joseph had seen the underside of two vehicles, not to mention the fire he first encountered. After verifying that Ben's transmission mount had indeed separated, Joseph had a go at fixing Tom's radiator leak. At one point in the day while we hovered over an engine, Joseph showed us how to listen to the internal workings using just a stick: one end on the engine, one end to the ear, just like a stethoscope. Suddenly, this whole new world opened up, one that exists underneath our hoods and yet goes unnoticed, sort of like Black Mesa. Most people I know in LA have no clue where Big Mountain is, or what problems the people are facing because of the coal LA and Las Vegas need in their thirst for energy. All of those blow-dries paid for with the blood of the Dineh and the earth, mind blowing, eh?

You would think that when people found out how much suffering goes on they would be horrified and rise up, demanding a new source of energy. To my growing horror of the human race, this is unfortunately not the case. Most ignore it, so they don't have to deal, or if they're slightly more humane they shake their heads and say, "that's terrible, but what can be done?" Even if you tell them what can be done, they shrug their shoulders and tell you their own personal list of problems. My faith in human kindness diminishes as my humanitarian work grows.

On Sunday we left two supporters on Black Mesa. One was staying for about ten days, and the other for just a couple more days. They would stay with two different families and help wherever possible.

At the same time we were making our rounds, Team 2, led by Autumn and Winter went to Big Mountain valley to deliver food and supplies. The families there were in desperate need of food donations and supporters on site to be witness to the ever-threatened impoundment and eviction process.

Eve Singer received four flats of dog food, a disposable camera and two boxes of food. Her daughter said that Eve was sent a grazing permit from the BIA, which stated she could have eight head of cattle, but it did not include her sheep. She has twenty-eight cows and one hundred sheep, so this is just an attempt to force her off the land. The BIA use the excuse that the land cannot sustain so many animals, but when elders corral the animals they show up armed and in force to impound the corralled livestock. So Eve didn't feel comfortable corralling animals because she does not trust that the BIA wouldn't come and take them from the pen. I can imagine these grown men sitting in their small lives, thinking up ways of harassing these old people and laughing at what they plan. Maybe I'm just thinking badly of people, but it sure seemed like they get a kick out of all of this. Since Eve's husband passed away she hadn't been feeling well; she was lonely and scared to stay alone at her place. She desperately needed a supporter who could help herd sheep, but there just weren't that many people who can dedicate months to that kind of commitment. She requested donations of livestock feed and dog food.

Team 2's caravan then went on to Hotevilla, where they dropped food to a Hopi family at the request of White Raven. They also dropped off boxes of food at Blue Star's for distribution to families in need: ten flats of dog food and six boxes of groceries. Harley Windstorm also received ten flats of dog food and ten boxes of food for his family. Blue Star made the most amazing traditional rattles, which he would like to sell more of. I always managed to buy something from him as I coveted them so much.

Years later, and to mark the new millennium, I decided to go on a wilderness fast in the hopes of uncovering some layers of my soul that had perhaps not been excavated yet, and with a desire to answer the endless question, "What is my life about?" I became part of a group called "The Condor Clan" that led wilderness retreats on a "giveaway" basis. They asked for no money, but you had to make some kind of donation to the community and of course fully participate in the meetings and pre-retreat exercises. My first night on the mountain I had taken Blue Star's spider rattle with me to use, and I sat on the side of the mountain overlooking the most incredible vista: mountains and forest stretching as far as the eye could see. It was a magical view cloaked in mist where you could easily forget that urban society ever existed. The sun was going down over the ridge, so I started to sing and "rattle down the sun." After a few minutes my heart started rapidly beating and it became difficult to sing. I stopped for a moment and tried to breathe deeply to calm my heart, but it didn't seem to want to take notice. Panic started to set in, so I started rattling again which just made the situation worse. The rattle was so powerful it had created a huge vibration my body couldn't handle, so I stopped. I was always very careful using that rattle again.

Team 2 was extremely lucky; they got to attend a Kachina Dance (a Hopi ceremonial dance performed by masked dancers embodying a Kachina) before they left Hotevilla for the long journey home to LA. Most Hopi ceremonies are closed to the public, so it's a rare privilege to be able to attend. I was quite jealous.

Team 1 delivered twenty flats of dog food to David Oaks for himself and to distribute to his neighbors, four boxes of food, toilet paper, and a variety of produce. David told us he would be moving to Sara Aspen's on Wed to help her out with her sheep. The elderly ladies were so strong and amazing, but life was really tough for them on their own. They did everything for themselves: haul water and tend sheep, which in itself is a full-time job and extremely physical work. I know hardly any white people who could endure such hardship and then have to deal with the brutality, intimidation and harassment from the Hopi Rangers.

At Peter Ash's house, we left ten flats of dog food for him to distribute, and two boxes of food for himself and a supporter who is staying with him. He also requested a passenger side leaf spring for his truck to get it running again. Without the truck, he couldn't haul water or food, so we added that to our wish list.

Five families on Low Mountain, all signers, received three boxes of groceries per family, five flats of dog food per family, miscellaneous fresh produce and toiletries. They also got children's clothes and some fleeces that Patagonia had donated. The families who signed the relocation agreement are called "signers." This means that when the elders of the families die they forfeit their hogans; their land and their children have to move either to the contaminated relocation lands or someplace else. Most of the families signed involuntarily, and although our main support goes to those families called "resisters" who refused to sign anything, it is hard not to feel compassion for people who barely understood what they signed and were coerced into doing so.

We visited six families total on Saturn Mountain including Jane Horsetail and Minnesota and Atlanta Storm. Atlanta said that her mother needed a female supporter with a vehicle. It was actually very hard to get people out to the land for support. Not only was it generally too rough for most, a lot of willing activists are poor themselves and don't necessarily even have a vehicle. I think that's why Ben and I were so popular: we had resources. Whilst all my other friends were buying houses and getting married, I was spending all my spare cash on Big Mountain. The families put in special requests for batteries size D, the large square lanterns, and of course more food.

Becky Lightning and her mother received twelve boxes of food, 60 flats of dog food, canned goods, produce, toilet paper and a disposable camera. The ladies said that after the United Nations Special Rapporteur on Religious Intolerance visited, a troop of twelve heavily armed Hopi rangers with an impoundment trailer came to their home and threatened to take away their livestock. This is generally the BIA modus operandi. They wait for all possible witnesses to leave and then start the retaliation harassment. The BIA doesn't want any interference in their efforts to relocate the Dineh.

Before Team 1 left we sat with David Oak in his Hogan. He wanted to dictate a memorial for his mother that we were to print. We had brought with us a picture of an elder that the Dorman web site needed permission to print, and, not knowing who it was, showed it to David. Amazingly enough it turned out to be his mother. We all sat in the main room of David's two-room house as the rising wind whipped against the plastic in the window. The window had broken, and they were trying to keep the weather out with a sheet of plastic, which wasn't very effective. We all kept our coats and hats on inside, as it was so cold. David was unable to make repairs to his house because of the Bennet Freeze. As he was explaining to me the story of his mother and I was taking down the dictation, he told us that he was a member of the Big Butt clan, and I couldn't help myself from stumbling. David kept repeating to me, "Big Butt, Big Butt!" and I was just staring at him helplessly thinking, I can't write that....the Big Butt Clan!! Everyone will think that's so funny, he then continued to explain that "butt" actually meant when two rams butt heads. I felt such an idiot.

His mother, April Robert Oaks, who lived Oct 30, 1923 – May 21, 1997, did a lot for her people and stood out as a voice for the traditionalists. She was a leader of the resistance and was arrested many times. David gave us the following statement for the Dorman page:

" My name is David Oak and I am "Where the Water Meets Together" and "Born for Edge Water" clans. My patrilineal clan,

is" Apache" clan. My matriarchal grandfather is "Many Goat" clan. We need all the support we can get at this time. We need to put pressure on the BIA, the Department of the Interior. We are threatened with losing our way of life by relocating to the outside world. It is very important that we preserve our culture and way of life. We can't live in the Western world. Our choices, our ways of life, being on the land, exercising our belief, and we don't want any U.S. Government interference with our life. This is on behalf of all the ways of Indian land in this hemisphere. We don't like human abuse, natural resource abuse that's happening in our nation. As we are all aware, as five-fingered family, we are all aware that we are losing our atmosphere and depletion of our ozone to where we are liable to sacrifice under the consequences. We all know that once everything was in balance and pure, now we all know it's out of balance. Climate, global changes are happening, it's here, greenhouse effect is here and these are my awareness and my concern. Then I think we are all in the same boat. So act now, pressure the U.S. government to tell them they are liable for it. That means industrial nation, fossil fuel addiction and nuclear addiction. And thank you very much."

It is without doubt that the Native Americans I met on the Hopi and Navajo reservations were warning us about climate change years before anything hit the headlines. Back then we didn't call it "Climate Change" we called it the "Earth Changes." I remember seeing the news on the front pages of the English papers one Christmas when I was visiting family. Whenever I had mentioned climate change to my mum she had, in her very English way, dismissed the idea as too far-fetched. Now it was plastered all over the front pages, and I remember grabbing the paper and shaking it at her saying, "See, it's true, it must be true, right Mum, if it's in the papers!" Of course, I was partly joking, as I sure as hell didn't believe everything I read in the papers, but Mum would normally assume it to be gospel. She just gave me one of her looks and moved on to the sweet counter. It's amazing to me that today, ten years later, global warming is now part of our daily narrative.

David told us that he needed willows and cattails to plant, and he mourned that the red sacred clay the Dineh called "tchi," which was used for pottery and sunscreen, was now gone due to the mine. All of the springs in the area had dried up, also thanks to the mine draining the aquifer for the coal slurry line. Peabody sucked up about two and a half million gallons of pristine water from the aquifer a day to transfer coal on its 273-mile long slurry line from the mine site to its power plant, the Mojave Generating Station. The coal plant was reputed to be one of the dirtiest in the Western U.S., and its emissions of sulfur dioxide and nitrogen dioxide poured out creating a haze over the Grand Canyon that stretched for a hundred miles.

It was getting really hard for them, and I mean really hard. David told us the story of how when the local families found out Peabody was going to destroy the area where the "tchi" was, all the families went over to the site with buckets to dig up as much as possible and hauled it away by hand. It occurred to me that this may have been why the Native Americans were called "redskins" on first contact, because the clay they used as sunscreen had either dyed their skin or they simply had the red clay applied to their bodies. David also asked us to get donations for gas money so he could take the local kids up to the Nevada test site for a Mothers' Day gathering with Corbin Harney and the Shoshone. Corbin Harney was the spiritual leader of the Western Shoshone people in Nevada and held a once yearly gathering of prayer, ceremony and peaceful actions opposite the nuclear test site that was situated on traditional Shoshone land.

It was time to leave, so James, Ben and I headed off in the direction of Red Lake to deliver seed to Grandma Silver Birch. We didn't really know the way to her home that well; I had never been and Ben had only been once or twice. Morgaine and Greystone Pine had to go someplace else to work, so we got a map from David Oak and tried to find our own way to the Silverbirch home. We turned off the main road at the Old White Mountain Trading Post and followed the pipeline down a very bumpy, rutted dirt track. We were hauling a trailer and wondering if we would make it. Eventually, we came to a gate that barred our way, so we stopped for a while to think about things. An odd sensation began to grow in my solar plexus, and I started to feel uncomfortable in the car as the boys talked, so I got out to get some fresh air, walk around and touch the Earth, which often helped to ground me. The wind had started to pick up and sing songs through the cliff formations, which lent to the steadily eerier-growing atmosphere. The canyon is a beautiful place, a deep wash, which obviously once held water. The rock formations resembled faeries castles, and I could feel spirits all around. There was animal medicine present, too. I bent down to say hello to the local residents at the entrance of a small critter's house under some brush. These are the times I feel the most "myself," when nobody is around to laugh or scorn me speaking to the animals and feeling the whispers of the spirits, just the Earth and me. As if for a moment I am suspended in a different dimension, the "real" one.

The wind picked up again, and the butterflies in my stomach were not calming down. I walked up to the barbed wire fence that stretched across the land whilst Jim and Ben continued to talk in the jeep. I hate barbed-wire fencing; it's so vicious, so made to hurt. Barely visible, you could run right into it; it divides animal's trails and is hard for them to see. They don't know how to step through it and not get caught up in its barbs. I raised my hand to hail my Mother Earth and Father Sun, and as I lowered it my far sight caught the glint of sun on metal. The reflection was from a parked truck, seemingly hiding from view behind a bluff. I went back to the car and told the boys. James got out of the car to check it out. Ever cautious of being watched by the Hopi rangers, we decided that the trailer would not make it anyway, and we all agreed it was time to go home.

I asked James to burn some sage, as my stomach was getting worse and the nausea was growing. The wind was really starting to blow hard and added to the incoming surreal feeling. We were all very alert and our nerves were taut like violin strings. As we bounced down the road, which wasn't helping my nausea, a large, white, swirling cloud appeared in the distance moving towards us. We stretched our eyes to try and see what it was. James said he thought it was another vehicle coming towards us kicking up dust. I looked harder and said,

"That's no vehicle, that's weather!" The storm rolled towards us like it was hunting the car, clouds heavy with snow. It was definitely time to go. I was sitting on the edge of my seat peering through the heavy fog that had suddenly enveloped us, watching the tumbleweed blow past. To everyone's great surprise an Indian man appeared out of the dust storm walking home, or walking somewhere, his jacket collar pulled tightly across his face, hat held on in the wind. I think my face drained of color and the boys fell silent as if we'd seen a ghost.

The subtle colors of the mountains were beginning to stand out as the storm blew in. The surrounding rocks looked intriguingly like cliff dwellings. I started to feel like I was in a Carlos Castaneda novel, and for some reason the appearance of the man so suddenly made my solar plexus swell with more agitation. Time slowed and all went quiet in the car as this surreal moment unfolded. My stomach was a plague of bees as the man walked past not even looking at us as I barely dared to look at him. The decision to head home seemed to solidify in everyone's mind at the same time, and the desire to leave became overwhelming. White clouds that rolled over the cliffs threatened snow. It felt like big medicine had put a stop to us delivering seed to Grandma Silverbirch. Well, we would get her the seeds another way. We had one more job to do and then we could head back to LA. There was an audible sigh of relief in the car as we made it safely off the dirt road onto tarmac and headed to Keams Canyon. Sometimes the strangest feeling can hit you on the mountain. I don't even know why or what it's about really. I just know it can hit anytime and anywhere. There is such strong energy up there, and the mountain seems to double the dosage of whatever you are feeling. Sometimes the pain was so intense, shards of glass seemed to be flowing through my veins.

We headed ninety miles east to Keams Canyon to photograph the impoundment yards and verify that no livestock was taken that week. We also wanted to identify and photograph Ruby Willow's horse, which had been taken the previous week. Ruby's horse seemed fine except for a gash on his head that had partly healed and did not look infected. It was hard to tell how old the wound was, but it certainly wasn't very recent. We then headed out back to Los Angeles. On the way home, using notes from Sally and Grandma Georgia, we began to outline the new supporters handbook for Georgia's family. The handbook, which was to be reviewed and updated by the Dineh elders, would be made available to all families to give to their supporters. It was to be a guideline concerning etiquette when staying with families on the mountain. The cultural differences between the Dineh and the people trying to help had become of concern for the elders.

Back in Los Angeles, at around the time we were heading home, a large crowd was gathering at a ceremony for the slain human rights activist Terry Frietas and his comrades at the home of Mary Wright in Malibu.

On the way home, we stopped off in Flagstaff for a clandestine meeting with Molly and Marigold from Black Mesa Indigenous Support group - BMIS for short. We met in a parking lot outside some shopping mall on a freezing, dark, wintry night. The ground outside was a skating rink of black ice. We climbed into the back of Molly's van to talk about the weekend, and what still needed to be done.

Luckily, Molly knew where Grandma Silverbirch lived and so we handed over the planting seed and asked that they make sure it got to her. I had bought these seeds especially for Grandma from an organic seed company that specialized in indigenous seeds of the Southwest, so I was very intent on them getting to her. It was very important to me, even before we knew about GMO crops, that if we were giving seeds to the Dineh, they should be indigenous organic seeds. It was as if the plants themselves could help heal the land and the people, and somehow disrupt the negative impact of the mining.

As the support groups were often out on the land helping, we gave them a verbal summary of which families did and did not receive supplies so they could attempt to fill in the gaps. We also discussed priorities and immediate needs, as well as the supporter's handbook material. We discussed contact information and debriefed them about our LA House of Blues event. Since we had thirteen hours of drive time to go, and a snowstorm was taking hold, we decided to cut the meeting short after an hour. To his credit, the BMIS dog was in attendance but said nothing. BMIS is an amazing group of young people who are always very supportive of our work.

After every run, we would send out a report to a website called the Dorman Page. It was always a very important matter to us that whatever we did, we also ensured that Greystone and Morgaine were recognized for their hard work. Without them, none of what we did could have been accomplished. It is endemic in our society that the people who are actually responsible for good work rarely get recognized, and it is invariable that some other person takes credit where none is due. Greystone and Morgaine worked tirelessly, leading us to all the families in need of help carrying with them a stack of legal paperwork to go through with the families. All the resisting elders that they visited would be given the latest news on Geneva and the BIA impoundments, and dozens of other issues that are of importance to the sovereign Dineh nation. Morgaine created an invaluable communications network which helped to keep everyone up to date. She would take down testimonies from the elders and their families that pertained to any type of human and civil rights violations. She would then later type up her notes and return to the elders, to verify them for accuracy and to be signed. Translators for these excursions have been numerous, including David Oak, Greystone Pine, Robin Aspen, Peter Ash, and family members of the elders themselves. It is a monumental task that must be done. In essence, this is how the case that went before the Human Rights

Commission was created. This exhausting pace Morgaine kept up seven days a week without any salary whatsoever. I hope one day the breadth and depth of her work is recognized, and I also hope that one day her work is published.

Around midnight on the long exhausting journey home, Ben, constantly frustrated by the lack of support, added for the Dorman Page report, "What do I need to do to wake everybody up to Morgaine? She eats, breathes, and sleeps this issue. She is bonded to these Grandmothers in a way that is unknown unless you follow her around. She is constantly under attack by people I never see on the mountain, and who do not have a clue what is going on at the Untied Nations. Anybody who has ears to hear, call me." This attitude seems to be indicative of the human race as a whole. People are very quick to criticize when they have no first hand experience of the issues. I guess it's their excuse not to get involved.

VIII

The Alders Weekend

On the way up to Big Mountain, we picked up some dehydrated food from Carol and Ellis Ray in San Dimas. Ben drove the Gaia Communications jeep, with a reporter from KPFK as his passenger. I traveled with Eric from San Cayentano Sweat Community in my little truck; Autumn drove with Arthur, Victor, and a photographer from the New Times. It's amazing how many of these groups don't exist anymore. The San Cayentano land was eventually sold, as Eric couldn't seem to make a profit from the orchards. This was such a great shame as it was a beautiful property, and he generously allowed many ceremonies and sweatlodges to happen on it. Perhaps it was his karma; I did hear his dark side used to get the better of him sometimes. The New Times paper eventually folded, which was another loss to the Los Angeles area for in-depth and alternative reporting. It was much more radical than the LA Weekly, and they were always very supportive of our work.

Grandfather and Grandmother Alder were two of my favorite Dineh. These two sparkling elders were the subjects of much recent and well-deserved love. Apparently none of the support groups have known about them for years, but now both the LA and Flagstaff support groups have found them, and had fallen in love with them. It was an old case of "If the elders don't want to be found they won't be," but now these two amazing people were in need of help. Grandma had been suffering with a serious cough for a long time, but Grandpa seemed in fine health. The house was in severe disrepair due to the Bennet Freeze, and in particular a corner of the ceiling had leaked during the rain and the insulation was hanging down. We felt that this added to Grandma's health problems, as the mould spores from the insulation were obviously floating around. Grandma had sat under this damaged corner for years, weaving and making her jewelry. Even now it brings tears to my eyes to think about that. The worst news however was yet to come, Grandpa told us that when he built the house for his family in the 70s he had collected what he called "pretty" rocks from all over the mountain, some of which came from the uranium mine he used to work in. They did not tell him how dangerous the uranium mine was or even that it was uranium, they just told him it was very "special" rock! I think we all turned pale at that news but refused to cry in front of them. We resolved to help them repair the house and somehow try and do something about the hot rocks without letting the authorities know. If the authorities found out the house had contaminated rocks in they would come and evict them immediately, and Grandpa didn't want that. It sounds crazy, but you had to respect his choice. After all, where would they go? This homestead was everything to them, and nothing was ever straightforward on the rez. A few months after finding all this out, we arrived to spend the weekend to help repair the house. I felt like this was my special project and one that I had advocated for from the beginning. I felt a very close bond, like many people did, with Grandpa and Grandma Alder. You could feel their amazing energy, and I so wished I had the courage or wherewithal to spend some more quality time with them helping them out and learning from them. It was a loss I was to feel all the more so years later after learning of the passing of Grandpa Alder. All of Grandpa's knowledge about local medicinal plants was gone forever, all of his wisdom, all of his songs. What a tragic loss, it breaks my heart still. In the last months of Grandpa's life, they moved to a trailer in Tuba City, as they just got too old to cope with the homestead by themselves, and Grandpa passed away. I guess the family didn't want to live in such an unsettled and remote environment anymore, so there was no one to take over for them. I still often kick myself for not just picking up and going out there for them so they could stay on the land. A huge loss for the Earth and for us all.

AIM had boldly and proudly delivered some sheetrock for us to use. Fantastic, except Grandpa already had enough sheetrock, and as always the AIM reps came up with plenty of excuses not to come for the weekend to help with the actual labor. This kind of thing happened a lot: people would arrive with donations that obviously made themselves feel very good, but the donations by and large turned out to be useless because they hadn't thought to ask what was actually needed. We did have a large caravan though; mainly writers and reporters who were also busy running around getting their stories and not able to help rebuild the house. I cannot express enough how much working with these elders made me feel at home and in sync with them. Actually pitching in to help and doing something constructive always got my respect before any verbal gratuity. Very judgmental of me I know; everyone has his or her job to do, but it annoyed me no end that able-bodied men seemed to do more talking and holding cameras than much needed physical work.

We arrived on Saturday morning after a long night of driving. Ben and the press team headed out across the mesa to deliver the food and complete some interviews for Victor and

The New Times newspaper. Autumn and her mother couldn't make up their minds what to do. We really needed them to stay at the house and help us, but Autumn had a crush on Ben so bad and really wanted to travel with him and the press team. Finally, and much to my annoyance because we needed all hands on deck for repairs, she decided to split the difference and go with Ben returning later to cook for everybody who had been working at the house. I just rolled my eyes and headed to the house.

Grandma had gone to Tuba City to stay with relatives whilst the house was being worked on, so Grandpa needed someone to cook for him, and there was too much work to do on the house and not enough people. It is so different dealing with the Dineh, when I asked Grandpa if he needed us to stay and help him with the house it is not in their custom to say yes, so he said no that's ok, he didn't need help. I don't think they can ask for help directly. For a moment everyone looked at me in confusion. This was a project that I had championed and felt compelled to help with. I figured that something cultural was going on, shrugged, and told everyone we were staying to help anyway. I found out later that it is not within their custom to tell someone directly what to do. You just have to jump in and then ask if it is ok to do something the way that you are doing it before they feel ok about giving advice. This has obviously led to much miscommunication between the Dineh and the supporters. Mind you, I think white people could benefit by holding off on to their desire to give advice so much when not asked!

The work was going to get really messy and toxic, so Fillmore Eric and I put on masks and goggles to start work on the house. Laboriously, we chipped up all the old tiles that were glued to the floor in the kitchen. We then took down the old ceiling and moldy insulation in the kitchen and replaced it, cutting and nailing up the sheet rock to make the new ceiling. We were told the generator one of the support groups had donated wasn't working, but by Sunday Eric had it going, so thankfully we could use the electric drills. After a long hard workday Saturday, the rest of the caravan arrived at the house to help finish up. We then went up to stay in Hotevilla for the night. I have never felt so exhausted in all my life, and was ready to utterly collapse. Every muscle in my body, and even a few I didn't know I had, was screaming from holding up sheet rock to the ceiling whilst Eric drove in the screws. My lungs were painfully complaining with all the dust and mold in the air; even though we wore masks, particles still got inside. God knows how much damage we were doing to ourselves, but even with all of that I have never felt so much gratitude for being able to help.

After dark, when we could no longer work, we rendezvoused with Ben and the press team in Hotevilla. Grandpa Alder couldn't handle so many guests with the house all broken up, so we had made arrangements to stay with Blue Star. Hotevilla was not built with cars in mind, so we had to park most of the cars up at Blue Star's main house, and then Ben, Autumn and I walked together down to the village house. Ben started to ask Autumn how the work had gone at Grandpa's house and what we had left to finish. I was totally incredulous as to why he was asking Autumn when she had barely been there, and had not picked up so much as a nail all day; she had done nothing but blither around and help her mum barbeque for us. This project was my baby, and I had coordinated all the efforts. She had no clue where we were or what needed finishing, so I could not fathom why Ben had chosen to act as if I was invisible, as if Autumn would know anything about the progress we had made. It was incredibly annoying and infuriating. I was so frustrated I couldn't do anything but stomp down to the village, fuming quietly. I felt that if I had said anything it would be made to sound like I was completely unreasonable and out of order. Ben was just doing it to give her attention, and it annoyed the fuck out of me.

Blue Star got us settled down in his little traditional house with fires lit and food being cooked. I loved to stay there; it was quintessentially Hopi and a real blessing to be able to stay in the middle of the village. His daughter Sage thought it was great every time we visit. I think to her we were the wacky people from the city, and our visit is something different that happens, so she had taken a shine to us and decided to sleep the night at the house too. This was good for us because we were still terrible at keeping the fire going, so it usually went out during the coldest part of the night and we all would wake up shivering. Sage could give us fire-starting instructions curled up in her bedding. Some brave person always had to get out of their sleeping bag and coax a new fire to start out of the embers of the old.

That night I had a very strange experience. Everyone was stretched out together on the floor tepee fashion, and I could hear the heavy breathing and light snoring indicating most people were exhausted and had fallen dead asleep. I was trying to get to sleep but having difficulty because my muscles were screaming so badly from all the manual labor. As I was thinking about how uncomfortable I was, the pain in my body seemed to intensify. A small panicky feeling welled up in my gut, which as soon as it had come, refused to go away. I could hear everyone's breathing get deeper as they slept. No one else it seemed was having that much difficulty after the hard work of the day. Anger and pain began to build inside of me, and I started to get frightened as it grew to an uncontrollable intensity. It felt like an outside force was present, around and inside of me. I hadn't ever felt so much intense anger before. My panic grew and I wanted to shout out to Ben, but everyone was sleeping and I knew I would sound crazy. Still the feeling inside of me grew, and I was beginning to spiral out of control. Maybe, I thought, there was something in the room that had this much anger, and I was feeling it in my exhausted open state. I felt sure my heart was going to give out, my throat constricted and I could barely breathe. Suddenly I felt a huge energy present that was larger than me, than all of us; it was here in the village, in the house, in all of the houses, and the epicenter of this strange vortex was right now hovering above the house that we were in. It acted like an amplifier over the whole village and could move at will. As the realization came into my mind that this energy of anger wasn't mine that it didn't belong to me, it suddenly stopped, as if someone had thrown a switch, and all the feelings of anger gave way. It was completely bizarre, and at that moment I realized that there was such bad medicine on the land it would act as an amplifier to any bad feelings you had inside of you. I think this energy turns people against each other and adds to the confusion and resentment so present in this battle against the coalmine. Finally, I was free to sleep and dream, and dream I did.

I dreamed that we had all woken up to find somebody or something on the roof of the house trying to get inside. It didn't appear to be very pleasant, so we had to barricade the doors and windows to stop it getting in. Much later that night Sage turned over and fell off the couch and landed on top of me. Obviously that woke me up! Weeks later I recounted the

Summer Crystalcrow feeding Georgia Pine's dogs

Mary Black's hand woven rugs

Rachel and James Silverbirches sheep

"Red Power Stop Relocation" graffiti on a water tank

Summer Crystalcrow and Muriel

Muriel feeds a stray

Unloading the semi truck

Setting up camp

experience to one of the Dineh who was visiting LA. She was utterly surprised and told me that the presence of this amplifying energy was true but no white people had ever felt it before.

We woke the next morning made some coffee and breakfast, and headed back to Grandma and Grandpa Alder's place. The press team helped us out on Sunday and did a great job. Ben and John started to dig the new outhouse. Autumn and her mother continued to cook and make coffee.

By the time we had to leave on Sunday to drive back to LA, there was still plenty of work to be done at the house. The stove had to be moved, and new floor tiles put down in both rooms. The ceilings and walls needed finishing touches. Both the living room and kitchen needed painting. The outhouse needed finishing. Two students from the Flagstaff support group stayed and worked at the house along with us. They were going to stay on and keep us informed of any work that may still need doing. Later, back in LA, we found out that Grandma Alder had visited the doctors during her stay in Tuba City and they had found a sore on Grandma's lungs. We were all very anxious to find out the exact diagnosis. I had often wondered about the uranium contamination in the house, and worried about it more as I worked in front of the rock wall that was guilty of coming from the uranium mine. Somehow I had no fear, though. Grandpa and I worked on the wall side by side; he was still so incredibly fit at over seventy years old. He had told me that he sings to the uranium rocks for protection against the radiation, and in that I found great relief and awe. All right, Grandpa!

The energy on BM is very strange; you feel it as soon as you drive onto the land, it is like a dome or a wall of energy that is heavy and thick. Silence always pervades the truck as you drive onto the rez. Your hearing becomes different, and things shift as if you wander into a different dimension, which looks exactly the same. The "medicine" lies like a heavy blanket across the mesas. That weekend was a particularly difficult one for me. I was in a great deal of physical and mental discomfort. I felt attacked from every side on a psychic level, as well as dealing with the radiation issue at Grandma and Grandpa Alder's, which was traumatic to say the least. I was extremely upset by this weekend and cried a lot when we arrived home. BM is always a strain, physically and emotionally.

IX

May 1st, 1999

The weather was good for the weekend run with Stefan, Autumn and Winter. The predicted blizzard at Flagstaff never really materialized - just snow flurries at worst. We arrived at Grandpa and Grandma Alder's house at 7:30am on Saturday after quite an eventful drive. Autumn and Winter had gotten into an altercation on the way up in the car over driving techniques, and they came to blows in a gas station on the I-40. Winter packed her stuff and took off down the road, determined to hitchhike back to LA. I was in the store paying and turned around just in time to see Autumn and Winter in a major confrontation by the pumps, screaming unheard words, and then Winter took off. I sent Stefan after her so I could finish paying but he couldn't find her, so we got in the truck and drove back down the road. There was a lot of heavy truck traffic around, as it was a major stop for the truckers. I was really concerned for Winter that she would just get in a truck and go home, and, more to the point, leave us a driver short which would be bad news all round. We eventually found her stomping angrily across the overpass, and after much negotiating to switch drivers around so she didn't have to drive with Autumn, we persuaded her to complete the mission.

Winter drove with me and Stefan drove with Autumn for the rest of the journey to Big Mountain. Luckily for me, they later made up their differences, so the next day Autumn and Winter were a team again, and took off to do the food run and take care of photos and interviews with Sara Aspen and Bella Whiteflower. I was extremely happy about this since Winter drove way too fast for me and I preferred Stefan's driving. Stefan and I stayed at Grandpa and Grandma Alder's house for the day. We painted the outside wood of the house, the kitchen walls and ceiling. Grandpa told me that people from Arizona University had come to take recordings of the uranium contamination in the rocks he built the house with. He said he saw the red light flash in a few places and the needle on the dial move up and down. He had initially thought that just one rock was the problem in the corner of the front room, but he had also seen these readings in the kitchen, too. I told him that after we had heard the results we would support whatever he decided to do with the walls in whatever way was necessary, but that we would discuss it with him and the other supporters to see what the best thing to do was. Unfortunately though, I never did find the people who took the readings, and they didn't return, so nothing was ever done. I wonder how many people the Dineh had encountered that promised to help in some way or another, and then never showed up again.

Grandpa had to take some of the old building material to the dump, so we loaded it in his old truck and I drove with him. Standing in the back of that truck with Grandpa unloading the trash was probably one of the best moments of my life. He stood there leaning on his shovel saying how lucky he was that he had so many friends. He said other people wondered why he had so many friends and people to help him, so I told him it was because he was a good man with a good heart and we all loved him and Grandma dearly. They had never been anything but kind, gentle, hospitable and welcoming to us, no matter how many strangers we turned up with. He invited all of us involved in helping him to his family gathering on Memorial Day weekend and said he considers us friends and relatives now. I politely had to decline, as I didn't think I could handle the sheep slaughtering ritual! I hope he wasn't offended. We left at sundown to meet Autumn and Winter at Blue Star's in Hotevilla to stay at the cottage in the village; I miss the Alders dearly.

At 9:00 am on Sunday morning we returned to Grandma and Grandpa Alder's to complete the finishing touches in the kitchen. Stefan helped Sean, a volunteer from Flagstaff, to finish off painting the wood trim outside. There were some things that still needed finishing. The outhouse needed finishing and painting; the kitchen cabinet needed moving and screwing into place; the front room needed sanding and painting; the doors needed varnishing; the windows needed changing and under the eaves outside needed painting.

Luckily, we had no harassment by the Hopi rangers. Grandpa had told me that the Hopi Rangers had visited him before to see if he had white supporters over at his homestead working, which was illegal!! Grandpa said he didn't talk to the rangers much - just told them he hadn't had anyone working there, and he thought the white supporters had gone elsewhere. I love how wily the elders can be when it comes to protecting those they wish to protect.

We returned to Hotevilla at about 1:00 pm to meet Autumn, Winter, and Ben, who was driving in from Colorado. It was good to see my brother, and he was glad to see us, he needed some cash for gas and knew I was probably one of the only people on the rez to carry enough cash for emergencies. We all made the long trek home to LA and arrived around midnight. Exhausted, I showered and fell into bed. None of the traditionalist has running water, so you can't shower. You have to heat water on the stove and wash, if you have time! By the time you get home, you're pretty stinky and dusty anyway. I am always so grateful to this day for the invention of the hot shower. It's not something I particularly want to live without.

X

June 19th, 1999

As part of a Gaia Communications mission, my friend Muriel and I left LA on Friday at 6:00 pm and headed to Big Mountain. We were going to check out and document Ruby Willow's cows and calves that the BIA had taken to the Winslow Ranch. Dean Gamble of the Hopi/Navajo land commission had previously told me on the phone that the animals were not impounded - merely being "held" for the families, pending decisions on their fate. They were taken from the families because the BIA had designated the Big Mountain land severely impacted by over grazing. This, of course, was incredibly laughable for a people who knew every stone, plant, bush and tree in their area. The Dineh would never do anything to the Earth that damaged its ecosystem, and if they did, certainly not as much damage as the cattle ranchers do to the land the BIA rents out to them.

I doubted that this was an effort founded in good intent as I had rarely seen any huge herds of cows or sheep on all of my trips driving around BM. The BIA had never previously demonstrated concern for the welfare of the environment or animals. We arrived in Flagstaff at around 3:00 am and slept for a couple of hours in the back of the truck parked in the Holiday Inn parking lot, right next to the old railway lines. We had to pee in the dirt behind the truck, hoping no one could see us which Muriel and I found hilarious.

We got up way too early and headed up to Denny's to meet Cathy, the animal rights lawyer from Plateau Lands Veterinarians in Flag. Unfortunately, she was very late because she had gotten mixed up and had been waiting at another Denny's. When she arrived to meet us, she was reluctant to head out to the ranch with us, but I wasn't going to let her go so easily as we needed her expertise.

We finally took off for the Winslow Ranch at around 9:30 am, an hour late to meet Morgaine and Ruby Willows. Needless to say, Wilbert Goy from the Land Commission had given us the wrong directions. Luckily, Morgaine was still waiting for us - albeit just about to give up, and complaining loudly. I was sure that Goy had deliberately given us the wrong directions, what an arse-hole. When we arrived, we went down to the corral where they were branding cows. The corral had no food or water and the cows and calves where in a terrible state. The Grandmas were clearly upset. We took photographs and video of Ruby Willow's cows that had been impounded, they all looked emaciated and sick. Ruby was extremely worried, as were we.

Her family told us there was one calf missing, and when they had asked Wilbert Goy about it he had responded by telling them he did not have time to look for missing cows. Other families also had calves missing; they were presumed dead or maybe even sold. One cow had given birth that day in the corral. From what we could see the land was in extremely bad shape. We documented as much as we could. The grazing was worse here then it was on Big Mountain, so it was obviously bullshit that the BIA took the cattle to protect the terrain on BM. The only available drinking water for the cattle was brackish, with dead frogs floating in it. It was awful, and Morgaine seemed to have given people the impression we were experts in animal welfare and were going to do something about the situation immediately. It made us feel extremely awkward, and I could see Cathy was totally overwhelmed. As much as I thought Morgaine's work was incredible, her exaggerations of who we were and what we could do were embarrassing and infuriating. It led to great disappointment with the elders, and they must have thought we were yet another group of white people who promised everything and delivered nothing.

Ruby Willow's family wanted to know where the veterinarian was and demanded to know what we were going to do about the situation; they wanted something done soon. I told them we would have to work on it, and there was nothing we could do that day except document everything as we had been asked to do. We discussed the situation with Cathy and decided to try and get a livestock vet she knew out to check out the cattle, and talked about how to address the animal abuse. Morgaine pleaded for Cathy's help. We also set a date for the Plateau Lands mobile spay/neuter clinic to come up to BM sometime in September, which was the earliest they could come. We would need to work on a location for them and how to get information to all the people. Muriel and I both made a commitment to be there for the first clinic to handle the animals and help get this going. We also talked about the need to return to the Winslow Tract with a veterinarian sometime in July when the families could return. I offered to stay in touch with Cathy and help.

We spent the rest of the day visiting with Morgaine and various families to discuss the Exclusion Order and the corral that needed to be built. Autumn was supposed to be helping organize the rebuilding of the corral the following weekend. Peter Ash and Sean Turtle, who lived on BM, offered their help, but neither had any transport and would need to be picked up.

It was, unfortunately, another situation that ended badly. We could neither find a veterinarian willing to take on evaluating the cattle nor persuade the mobile spay/neuter clinic to come up to the rez. There were numerous obstacles that thwarted us, but it turned out to be the location more than anything. The spay/neuter van needed a stable location, and could not travel dirt roads. The only plausible location would have been the mine, and for that to happen we would need the cooperation of Peabody, which would never have happened. Plus, it would have involved a huge effort coordinating communication to people who had no phones and getting transportation to the homesteads to pick up the animals - something we would need a number of vehicles for. As for the corralled animals, we would have needed to bring our own horses to round up the cattle for inspection, and that also meant the co-operation of the BIA, which would never happen. Organizing horses, trailers, vets and the BIA was completely beyond our resources, but I wish Morgaine hadn't promised people that we were going to do something about the cows before we could really figure out the logistics. It was a huge mess and far too big a project for our resources and manpower, much to my great disappointment.

Cathy went back to Flag, and we took Morgaine back across the mesa to Big Mountain. Ben had given me a message to deliver to Morgaine about the receipts for the SDN accounts. He had gotten mad at some missing receipts and wanted to know what had happened to them. I gave her the message, which ended up being a complete can of worms, as we then had to listen to her ALL afternoon going on and on about it. Morgaine could be the most unbelievable broken record sometimes. She cried and threatened to cut Ben off and lose him as a friend altogether. I understand her being upset, but man; I had had enough of her obsessing about the same subject all day. It seems to me that everyone had reached his or her maximum stress level. To this day Muriel and I still joke about the day Morgaine talked about "reeeeeeceipts" incessantly.

Morgaine asked me to call Ben and speak with him because she didn't want to talk to him herself but had something to say, so we stopped at the store on Second Mesa to make the call from the public phone. Then after refusing to speak with him when I was on the phone, she said he'd missed his chance because she was prepared to speak to him after I had hung up! Jeez louise, what an impossible woman she was! We took off again, back to Black Mesa, and visited David Oak to photograph the wrecked truck for the insurance people. Ursula, from the Fillmore Sweat Lodge, had donated a truck, but Tina had rolled it into a ditch. It was totally screwed. Peter was there, but David was at a ceremony. That was good for us as word had it he had been drinking lately and after the Will Nightshade experience I can do without any more drunk drama. Morgaine took us over to Robin Aspen's, but she wasn't at home, so we went to Esther and Kevin Sycamore's. Morgaine wanted to show them she had received an exclusion order as well. Arlene Hamilton, who was currently living up at the Witness Camp, had also received an exclusion order.

I like Esther Sycamore very much. The last time she had stayed at my house she had given me a beautiful pinon nut necklace in thanks for my hospitality. I really love the pinon nut necklaces - somehow they are imbued with Grandmother energy and I feel very protected when I wear them. I would like to help Esther more. She is one of the Elders that have the most wonderful warm, bright, loving light around her. The wrinkles in their faces speak volumes of wisdom and kindness. We next went to visit Ken Acorn and his wife to tell them volunteers would come next weekend to build their corral instead of this weekend. Their very good-looking, son, Acorn was there which raised both our eyebrows. He seemed quite keen on the gorgeous Muriel. A few years later Winter became his partner, and they had a child together. It was, of course, a tumultuous relationship that didn't last. The boy child was eventually shipped off back to the rez to live with his grandparents as neither parent could cope. I heard that Winter later took him back trying to sort out her life and become a mother to him again.

Young Acorn wanted both of us to return to build the corral, but I wasn't about to make that commitment right then, especially as the corral building was Autumn's project. I wanted to stay out of that mix as much as possible. Next on our agenda was to find a beautiful, peaceful place to watch the sunset, relax and smoke some herb.

As the three of us were heading back home we pulled off the road and drove down a small, pretty, sandy canyon. We sat around for a couple of hours talking, smoking and watching the light fade into darkness. Morgaine told us the story about her time helping to reintroduce the wolves to Yellowstone Park, and how she got to actually run with the wolves. This was just fascinating to me. I am so in love with wolves, what they stand for and how gorgeous and mysterious they are. After a while, we decided to take off as it was getting dark, and we jumped back into the truck. As I turned the truck around I drove off the dirt road a few feet, and suddenly we were chewing sand big time. The truck had sunk like the Titanic. Freak out time! It got really bad in a matter of minutes, and our euphoric mood turned sour instantly. It took two seconds for us to get stuck and the next hour to dig ourselves out. We were in the middle of nowhere and Morgaine was panicking. She started walking around the truck, smoking furiously, saying, "This is really bad, really bad!" And then she suggested we walk to the mine to get Greystone. What a crazy idea; the mine was at least twenty miles away and would be one helluva walk on a dirt road in the dark. Muriel saved the day by being the total Taurus she is and she became determined to dig us out. She managed to stop me freaking out by boldly stating,

"Don't worry Summer, if I have to dig a new fucking road I'll dig out this truck." That calmed me down, so we both got down on our hands and knees to dig the wheels free. It looked like an impossible situation, as the truck had sunk up to the axle. Then Muriel had the presence of mind to use the planks of wood that always live in the back of my truck. Lord only knows why I carry them; call it divine inspiration.

As we dug we tried to shove the boards under the wheels. Ominous clouds were rising over the horizon and lightning was starting to streak the sky. I looked around and noticed to even more dismay that our peaceful retreat off the road was actually a riverbed, and I could only imagine the worst. As thunder rolled overhead, I envisioned a flash flood coming down the creek bed and wiping out the truck - then we would really be fucked. As mild panic took up residence in my belly, I realized much to my horror that my visions of doom were not beyond the realm of possibility on Big Mountain. I had heard many a story of similar situations turning into disasters, with people's vehicles being washed away by flash floods.

After an hour of digging and a lot of sweat and prayer, we freed the wheels enough to push the truck out, tearing away the exhaust in the process. I was never so relieved in my life! I didn't think we were ever going to get the truck out of there. Well Muriel, god bless her, was the heroine of the moment. Her logical Germanic mind and her stubborn determination kept us digging through sweat, panic and broken nails. Unfortunately, I later found out we tore the muffler, and certainly the transmission was damaged. Oh well, the old faithful little truck was still well enough for us to drive back to Kaibeto and save us from a night either walking to the mine, or sleeping rough and then walking to the mine. That night we stayed in Greystone and his wife's five-star hogan. Although not completely working, it had a shower and air conditioning, a complete kitchen, and best of all a nice big double bed for Muriel and I to rest our weary heads on. It was a warm evening with a nice breeze blowing the spirits around; perfect for the last night, and boy were we glad for it.

I woke up early the next morning and day-dreamed of turning over to find a man wearing nice brown skin and long black hair lying next to me, only to turn over and find Muriel snoozing away! Bah humbug. So I went back to sleep as it was way too early to get up. Muriel and I finally rose about 8:00 am, and we wanted to split quickly. Morgaine tried to delay us with phone calls, cigarettes and demands, but I made Muriel promise me that I could blame her for our quick departure with some excuse of having to get back to LA. When we walked into the Greystone's house it became a bit awkward as Rebecca, being Navaho and extremely hospitable, had expected us for breakfast, but we wouldn't have gotten out of there for hours if we stayed. Greystone greeted me with a huge smile, which was really nice. It was a shame and a bit rude of us, but I really wanted to get home at a reasonable time, and I think by then both Muriel and I were ready to leave. We made our pathetic excuses, left and grabbed coffee and doughnuts on the road. I'm sure they just shook their heads at our crazy "bahanna" ways. It was an absolutely stunning morning, and Muriel and I were in jubilant spirits.

On the way to Tuba City, we passed a cute Indian kid hitchhiking, so we stopped to pick him up. Poor thing had been waiting in the sun for three hours and was only about fourteen years old or so, but I think we made his day by sitting him between two blonde bahannas from LA. We fed him doughnuts and water and got him talking. He pulled out an amazing turquoise necklace from his pocket to sell, which I bought for Tina's birthday. It was a lot of heavy turquoise for thirty dollars, but he ended up with forty anyway. He started regaling us with stories of skin-walkers, which are some of my favorite old wives' tales. He told us not to walk around at night because the skin-walkers were dangerous spirits, and the only way he knew how to kill them was to take a feather from their hair, if you can get near enough to them that is, he added menacingly. Muriel and I feigned horror and surprise, which encouraged him even more to tell us about the night his uncle stopped to pick up an old woman standing by the side of the road. Apparently, his uncle knew she was a skin-walker because she had a withered arm, a hunchback, one leg and a tail like a donkey. Well, I would have never guessed she was odd! Muriel and I could barely contain our laughter. Apparently, the old lady sat in the back of the truck and said nothing. After a while, his uncle grew uncomfortable with the silence, but when he turned around to talk to her she had disappeared! What a fantastic story! We were having a thoroughly good time.

Prompted to continue his fable telling by our exclamations and goading he told us another story of the night his Grandpa and sister were out walking. His sister grew tired and somehow lost one of her shoes. So the Grandpa gave her a piggyback, and when they got home there was the shoe sitting in front of the door! His Grandpa had also told him not to pick up crow feathers (oh dear, I have a collection of crow feathers at home which are my very favorite birds) but he didn't say why. He told us they used to kill crows for attacking the cornfields. How terrible! I couldn't believe that someone would kill such awesome creatures, and I was very disappointed to hear that. As we drove past a large body of water, he pointed over to it and told us how there had been numerous drownings in the lakes by Tuba natural springs. I'm sure the lake must have a hazardous undertow, but on the rez it became a supernatural occurrence. Our story-telling hitchhiker was such great fun; we dropped him in Tuba and continued on our way home, laughing at his stories. I'm sure he regaled his friends with his amazing story of the two hot bahanna chicks who picked him up and fell for every word he said, and I bet his friends didn't believe a word of it. It was good energy all round, although I did wonder how he actually came by the necklace.

Muriel and I couldn't resist stopping at Joe Cody's jewelry stand on the drive home. There are large signs posted at intervals for about a mile down the road before you get to the stand: "Chief Yellow Horse Jewelry Stand," "Stop now at Chief Yellow Horse," "Don't pass Chief Yellow Horse," "Next stop Chief Yellow Horse." Of course, Chief Yellow Horse was nowhere around, but I did wonder if they didn't mean "Chief Yellowcake" since we were horribly close to the area in which Ben had previously detected high levels of uranium contamination with a Geiger counter. Chief Yellow Horse turned out to be Joe

Cody, from whom I bought a gorgeous knife with a turquoise handle. It cost a lot of dough and I probably got completely ripped off, but I had to have it. Muriel bought some necklaces as presents for friends back home. The rest of the journey passed pretty peacefully although we consumed way too many cigarettes and doughnuts, (the food of champions), eventually arriving back in LA around 9:00 pm. Phew!

XI

June 25th Run

Ben and I drove up to Big Mountain on 25th June 1999. We decided to do a quick run, so just took one truck. We arrived in Flag early in the morning, and camped out for a few hours just outside Seligman to wait for Cathy from Plateau Lands Veterinary Clinic. We wanted to get an interview with her on video talking about the animal situation up on the rez. She arrived on time with a friend, and we chatted for a while to get more acquainted. Ben filled her in with more of the big picture of BM. She seemed such a nice person; I hoped we could rely on her for help. That day, I learned from Cathy that there is a research unit in Flagstaff that experiments on dogs and other animals for Gore-Tex. I was absolutely horrified; I didn't realize that they tested animals for new clothing products too! She told me that one of the technicians had felt so badly for one of the dogs she rescued him, but the Feds caught up with her two states later. It turns out they put tracking devices in the dogs to make sure they can recover the dogs if anyone decides to rescue them from their horrible fate. I can hardly believe it; they are Josef Mengeles gone mad! I will never buy Gore-Tex again.

After saying goodbye to Cathy and her friend, we drove up to Hopi Village to visit Blue Star. He wasn't at home, but we found him at a family gathering and of course, according to the amazing Hopi hospitality, we were immediately offered food. We chose coffee and pie and sat down to eat. His wife Opal and daughter Sage were there. It was really good to see them. Sage has this quirk where she wants two of anything you offer her. It's very funny, when you give her something she always asks, "Only one?" And then looks at you with huge brown eyes. I always gave in and ended up handing her two: one for each hand. After visiting with Blue Star, we went to see the village Kikmongwi. (Kikmongwi is the Hopi term for the village chief.) He was funny too! He was wearing a pair of shorts that well… could have been longer really, and I was trying very hard not to laugh at them. I had to keep looking at other things around the house. Somehow it just didn't fit my expectations to see a traditional Hopi, with the basin haircut they favor, wearing modern clothes, especially shorts! He told us he didn't plant any corn this year because he didn't think it was going to be a good year.

"No rain," he said, "too hot. Summer is going to be short this year, nuh!" He eyeballed me suspiciously, rubbing his knee. I suppressed another smirk and studied the pictures on the wall. Ben spoke with him about other things, but I was way too distracted to focus on what they were discussing.

Afterwards, we continued down to Coal Mine Mesa to visit Grandma Eucalyptus, who had broken her wrist. I was very concerned, as her wrist looked swollen and painful. I must remember to bring her painkillers on the next run. We gave her some blankets and a few clothes. Grandma Eucalyptus is now in her BIA house. She looks so out of place, but I think the dugout became a little rough for her. What she really needed was a nice, comfortable new hogan. Maybe I'm wrong and the house is good for her, but right now it doesn't look lived in. The BIA house is too new and stark, unlike the natural coziness of a wood hogan. Or maybe it just doesn't seem to fit a traditional Dineh to live in a square house with painted white walls, just like new clothes don't seem right on a traditional Hopi.

We left Grandma Eucalyptus with our usual feeling of inadequacy and hopped over to her neighbor Ruby Willow. Ruby wasn't at home, so we headed off to another Hogan, but Ruby came driving to find us in her big old truck, blue plastic water barrels bouncing in the back. She must have spotted us from quite far away with her all seeing, shiny black eyes.

Through gestures, broken English, and pointing at the calendar we talked about trying to get a veterinarian up with the next caravan on 25th July. Seeing as it was so difficult to get anyone like a vet up to the rez, we settled on picking her up that weekend and going down to where the BIA had taken the impounded cattle. We would take cattle food with us, and that made Ruby Willow seem much happier, she was so worried about her animals, they are like family to her.

After visiting with Ruby, which is always such a delight for me as she usually has baby lambs in the hogan, or some other creature who has come to her for help, we headed to Monument Valley to get some scenery for the documentary.

Monument Valley is absolutely stunning and one of the places I visited when I first arrived in the States, but there was nowhere to camp, so we headed back to Red Rock to find somewhere to stay for the night. Big mistake, we should have found somewhere on Big Mountain. Ben was driving down into Grandma Silverbirch's canyon and drove off the road to camp, where we promptly sank up to the axle in the sand. We tried and tried to dig the truck out, but she just wasn't having it. Ben insisted he knew how to dig us out, and I insisted we do it the same way Muriel had gotten us out a few weeks earlier, all to no avail. We were as two stubborn goats arguing. So with both of us in a terrible mood after failing miserably, we gave up to wait for morning, and camped where we were for the night. I sat on the ground to sulk and Ben complained I was sitting in sheep's dung, and it would be disgusting in the truck, which made my mood worse. Eventually, we found our sense of humor and Ben managed to make me laugh. I don't know whether I actually saw the funny side of my truck being, yet again, stuck up to its axle in sand, propped up precariously by the jack, but there really was nothing else for it but to put it down to another Big Mountain experience.

In the morning we elected Ben, since he was the one who drove off the road into the sand, to walk the long three or four miles back to the store to get help. I watched him disappear down the dusty track, looking like a latter day version of Kokopelli, shoulders hunched against the inevitable long trudge. I made some coffee and started burning sage to pray. I settled in for the long wait, but it seemed like only moments till Ben returned with a tow truck. What an amazingly welcome sight that was, and so quick! Thank goodness for Ben's easy, amicable approach to people, who always warm to him immediately. If I had gone it would have probably turned into some weird, easy prey, stranded female situation anyways. It's not a good idea for women to drive around alone on the rez, especially if they are not locals and so obviously not Indian.

After that entire escapade, my truck popped out easily with one good tug. Ridiculously enough, we ended up towing the tow guy down the road, as he then broke down after getting us out! With our stupidity still in full working order, we decided it would be a great idea to drop the ecstasy we had brought with us, and headed off to the Grand Canyon to see if we could enjoy the rest of the day.

Second huge mistake of the weekend, or so it seemed later! Unfortunately, the 'E' hit me like an express train gone wild, and I hit the deck of the truck and could barely move for hours, becoming more incomprehensible with every passing minute. Ben pulled over, and I fell out of the truck and onto the dirt hoping it would help to ground me. The earth, though, had other ideas; it was vibrating with tremendous energy, which was shooting through the palms of my hand all the way up my arms to my heart, which was now answering by rocketing along. I couldn't stand properly, but my mind was screaming 'keep moving'. I mumbled to Ben,

"Let's go, let's get out of here" and dragged myself back into the truck. We headed for the Grand Canyon, where I had to borrow Ben's shades because mine weren't big enough for my paranoia, and quickly became horrified at all the huge, white, American tourists in their extremely loud shirts. I grabbed Ben's hand to navigate the parking lot, but he was getting seriously annoyed with me and shook me off like an errant child.

I felt horribly vulnerable and terrified. We managed to walk some ways down the narrow path on the side of the canyon along with the other tourists, but I took one look over the edge and that was it. I fled or rather crawled, clutching the side of the mountain back up the path to the truck. Talk about "Fear and Loathing" in the Grand Canyon! I insisted we keep driving, and Ben, who had had quite enough of me for one weekend, was happy to oblige. As we drove, the wind began to speak with me and gave me a vision. The 'E' blew a door wide open in my mind, and the wind hurtled into it from Monument Valley. It began to tell me that I was the Prophetess, but wasn't strong enough yet to open to the energy that was there. The wind told me to do more ceremony to make my body and mind stronger, and that the earth elementals were too powerful for me to converse with now; they would blow me apart if I tried. My soul became a battleground, and my body was wracked with pain. On one side, I felt that it was my ego playing games which had been bolstered by the drug, and this was all nonsense; I couldn't possibly be anything worthy. The other side felt dejected because I had been rejected, just like my first experience with Monument Valley, where I had such a horrible experience camping with a friend but had seen visions in the clouds.

The wind talked of many things to me: it spoke of a destructive wind that had been loosed from its holding tower and was coming to do something in the world. It spoke of how the world had become corrupt, and now the earth elementals were coming to help put balance back into the world, and the wind was its warrior of change. They gave me the vision and I could see the ruined stone tower, sitting on the slopes of dusty mountains on the edge of a vast desert, with a great wind moving about. Many years later I read basically the same thing that the vision had shown me, the wind being freed from a tower to come balance the world, in the book of the Hopi, Hotevilla. It was an amazing revelation.

Ben tried to help and get me to sit up but it was no good; I felt worse if I tried to cut the wind off from talking to me. I had to get off that land, fast. If I did not leave, I felt like I would die or end up in the loony bin, dribbling in the corner somewhere. I just wanted to go home.... so we did. It was a hard drive back to LA. Ben was upset that I had taken so badly to the 'E' and couldn't talk to anyone but the wind for hours! I felt dreadful, as if I had completely ruined everything. Years later, I would again encounter another wind on a vision quest but that's another story.

XII

August 1st, 1999

My neighbor Stephanie and I set out from LA around 2 pm on August 1st in my faithful little grey and white truck. It was a nice, uneventful drive apart from the awesome landscapes that slowly faded from city to desert to mountains and we encountered no turbulence. We arrived at Big Mountain at about 2 am and promptly got lost on our first foray to find Georgia Pine's house. Her home is a tricky one to see in the dark, not that any of the Dineh homesteads are easy to find, but Georgia's doesn't have any noticeable markers by the dirt road. We were both really tired, and weren't as attentive at marking the mileage off on the map on the first time in and missed the turnoff.

Stephanie was still the novice Big Mountain visitor, so she just kinda looked confused when I asked her if she had kept track of where we were on our homemade map. I was very tired, and my moontime had arrived, which compounded my irritability. In fact, I was too tired to work out the math on the mileage, so the only thing I could think of to do without getting us more messed up was to go back to the gas station and start all over again. So many people get lost driving around and around in the daytime, let alone at night, thinking they can figure out how to get to people's homesteads, and I was way too tired to deal with being stranded all night or ending up with the truck stuck in some ditch again. We found the right dirt road the second time in, with Steph rewriting the map to a more accurate mileage, and both of us intensely checking our progress every few miles. We pulled up into Georgia's driveway at around 3 am, and quickly emptied the truck of all the supplies we had brought with us so we could sleep in the back. We were both so tired we passed out as soon as our heads hit the pillow.

After twelve hours of driving, a sleeping bag and pillow in the back of a truck feels like a luxury. Funnily enough, when we woke in the morning we had both had similar dreams. Steph dreamt that there were many spirits around us trying to confuse us. Mine was a little more vivid. I dreamed that there were many spirit people around staying in the hogan and around Grandma Georgia's. Simon English, who was my long time school friend, was also there. He had recently died in a fairly mysterious way back home in England. He had drowned the week prior off the south coast in our hometown of Lymington, and I was still mourning him. In my dream everything was moving fast; the spirits moved as quickly as the wind. Simon was having a good time in the spirit world and had come to the mountain to help me. In the dream, Simon and I went into Georgia's hogan, which had a lot of people in it. Simon became very agitated at one spirit sitting in an armchair facing the wall. He sensed danger and warned me to leave. He became extremely frightened as the man in the chair started to turn around, and shouted at me to run. Simon fled the hogan very scared, running as fast as his spirit legs would carry him. I started to run, but looked back and caught a glimpse of the strange man. He had dark hair and very piercing eyes. He was grinning at us in a strange, unnerving way, so I continued to flee following my spirit brother.

We woke up bright and early, threw everything back into the truck and drove the short distance to Morgaine who was staying in a new place. The Pines had put her in Greystone's trailer, which was parked up the hill from Georgia's house. As we were driving past, Georgia appeared at the door of her house and ominously beckoned us in, so we had to stop. Unfortunately, her daughter Sally was there as well. Sally used to be our friend and translator, but now she regaled us with gossip about Morgaine, saying how she only liked men to take her around, and how they used to be good friends but now Morgaine only wanted men!! Sally told us that Morgaine even had young men go in and out of her place, and no one knew what was going on anymore.

Oh dear! I could care less how many men Morgaine chose to have in her home, but I did not believe Sally's malicious gossip. It was hardly Morgaine's style anyway. I just felt extremely uncomfortable and wanted to leave. It was highly unlikely that Morgaine stopped talking long enough to entertain strings of men. She was such a chatterbox, and probably the young men Sally was talking about were bahanna activists who needed to talk with Morgaine. The cultural divide just grew larger at that moment, right there in Georgia's front room with Sally's gossip. I also realized that the proverbial shit about Greystone and Morgaine's illicit relationship had started to hit the fan. Stephanie was just stunned that a Navajo woman could be so harsh and terrifying, but more's the pity, they are not always spiritual and wise. We left Georgia's house as soon as we could make excuses to get out and headed up to the trailer. Little did I know, but that was the beginning of the end.

Morgaine, as usual, was extremely chatty and happy to see us. I didn't bother to inform her of the gossip, as I knew this would upset her greatly and served no purpose. I also didn't want to spend the day listening to her endlessly haranguing me about it as she was wont to do, so it was best to keep quiet all round.

After a cup of coffee or six, we finally got the ever-talking Morgaine into our truck so we could get going on our mission. We took off to pick up David Oak to translate for us on our rounds. When we got there, we discovered the medicine man had come by already and taken David and Peter off to a ceremony. Archie and Tina were home in David's house, so we hung out for a bit, waiting. I grew tired of this, thinking we could wait for days for someone on the rez, so Archie and I went down to the hogan to see about David. He eventually came outside and said they had only just started praying to the second direction and so could still be a couple of hours. A couple of hours is Dineh speak for all night, so I wasn't about to wait any longer! It was getting late so we headed off to find Robin Aspen to help translate instead. Robin is about thirty years old with an alcoholic husband and five kids. She also has kidney failure, and every five weeks or so drives the fifty miles to the nearest dialysis machine. The people in charge of the transplant list at her hospital won't put her on the kidney transfer list because she doesn't have a telephone of her own. We caught up with her on the way back from the store, loaded up her truck with some bottled water we had brought, and finally started our rounds of visiting. Robin was married to a man I did not trust at all. Apart from the fact that he was a drunk, he always looked like he was planning some mischief. I always locked the truck around him. I didn't even trust he wouldn't run off with the water we just handed over, and sell it to buy booze.

Our next stop was Lisa Nielson; she wasn't at home, but her obnoxious brother was. He was about forty years old, slightly overweight and very grumpy. You could see it on his face, and the way he looked at you as if he was disgusted with you. He probably was because we were white. He invited us into the hogan and we all sat down at the table. As is traditional with the Navajo, he offered us something to eat, but unfortunately, it was mutton stew. When he went to give me some, I said,

"No thank you, but I will take some coffee." He got outraged at this and started to shout at me that I was a rude and ungrateful bahanna. He thrust a bowl of mutton stew at me and said,

"You eat it." Of course, I wasn't about to eat meat for anyone and was not easily intimidated by an angry Indian man. I stared at it and then looked back at him.

"No thank you," I replied, " I don't eat meat" and pushed it away. Morgaine grabbed the bowl and hoping to diffuse the situation said,

"I'll eat it." He glared at me but sat down, and he and Morgaine started to talk about the situation. His bahanna supporter then got up from the table and came back holding some rice dish, which she gave me and spoke softly

"I don't eat meat either." I smiled warmly at her and began to eat it. Dark thunder face continued to glare at me as he listened to Morgaine. After we had visited for a while, we drove to Black Mesa and ended up at Ruby Willow's.

We had gone the long way round, making a stop to buy "medicine" in Hotevilla. We had wanted to visit Blue Star, but the homecoming dance was being held, and if the Hopi rangers caught Morgaine she would probably get detained on the spot. Morgaine was on the top of the Hopi rangers' most wanted list. On the way down from Hotevilla to Coal Mine Mesa, we drove off the road a little ways and stopped to smoke. Robin told us a little bit about White Shell Woman, as the area we were currently parked in was apparently her home. We hid the truck behind some brush on a dirt track off the main road, surrounded by low-lying sandy hills that were beautiful voluptuous mounds. White Shell Woman is one of the Chief Goddesses who plays an important part in the creation myth of the Navajo. Sister of Changing Woman, and sometimes considered the same Goddess, she was impregnated by the Sun or a mountain stream, depending on which myth you read. She gave birth to the heroic Slayer Twins who slayed monsters.

After what seemed like hours we finally left, because of course the girls wanted to smoke loads and Morgaine never stopped talking. We didn't actually get to Ruby Willow's until the sun had set, which made the drive down to her extremely precarious. Ruby lives in a ruggedly beautiful canyon, but to get to it you have to go down an incredibly steep dirt road, which is only the width of one car. The drop on one side is all the way to the bottom of the canyon, which wouldn't be pretty. If there is more than one car you have to go down one at a time. Coming back up is even better; you have to take a run at it to make sure you don't slide back down, especially in bad weather. It's quite scary. I however, thoroughly enjoy this mad driving; I swear I missed my vocation as a rally driver.

When we reached Ruby's Hogan, her extended family was visiting. Her grandson was getting married next week in New Mexico, and as they were all going they had come over to make arrangements to take Ruby with them. I found out later that Ruby's children were all adopted. She had thrown her husband out for drinking a while ago, and I guess they never had kids of their own. What a remarkable mother she must have made. Incredibly strong for such a petite lady, she could outrun all of us, even in her seventies. Ruby was very traditional, had a lovely cozy hogan, and was extremely bonded to her animals. Her small dark eyes always shone, and she had one of those beautiful, weathered faces with so many lines and wrinkles that hold so much Earth wisdom. One of those most remarkable magical women who will, for the most part, pass from this world unnoticed except for by her kin, her animals, and the Great Mother herself. A very powerful woman who was truly connected to the earth. She once proudly told us of a time when the Hopi rangers had come to harass her, and she had met them defiantly with a loaded shotgun and ran them out of the canyon. I have that image of Ruby burned into my brain: shining black eyes, hands on hips; laughing as she recounted the story to us. There are so few of the Dineh Grandma's left.

Poor Ruby became visibly distressed when we reported to her what the vets had said about her cows being held on the BLM land. I was so sorry I could not have done more for her. She said she wanted her cow's home; that they were as much a part of the land as she was. They would be missing seeing her every day, and she was so worried I feared she wouldn't sleep all night. My heart went out to her.

Never have I met a woman who is so close to her animals; she has so much love and respect for them and their place in the natural order of things. Ruby was always caring for small birds and other creatures; she had such a strong connection to all of her animals. We could learn so much from her, but alas the human condition in these times knows no compassion or respect for each other, and less for the other creatures on this planet. I have never heard anyone speak so heartfeltedly about the animals in her care, and speak about their feelings and needs too. What was happening always makes me sad; listening to Ruby my heart grew even heavier, as I share her love and respect for the animal kingdom. What hell hath man wrought upon our sacred ground? Sometimes I can hardly bear it. We really wanted to help in some way, so we discussed taking her to meet the vets the next week at the Winslow ranch, and I agreed to pick her up Sunday morning. We then bid our goodbyes, all of our hearts much heavier with sorrow for Ruby and her cows.

I was starting to hit the wall of exhaustion, so after I had driven us out of the canyon up the steep treacherous road, because of course I wouldn't trust anyone else to do that, Steph took over driving. I was always paranoid about that section of road. I wonder how my little two-wheel drive managed most of what I made her do. We have definitely driven over hill and dale together, and she has been amazingly trustworthy. That little truck is imbued with the spirit of adventure, how many stories it could tell! As I dozed in the back of the pickup, I felt us hit the dirt road again and started getting anxious. I had asked Steph to wake me and let me drive on the dirt roads, because if we got stuck then I would only have myself to blame, and my temper is notoriously quick. Well wouldn't you know, she decided I needed the rest and wanted to let me sleep, which was very sweet of her. With Morgaine and Robin watching passively, Steph went to skirt around a huge puddle that stretched across the road, and the truck sank immediately in a foot of mud, coming to a sudden halt. Of course, it is the Dineh way not to give advice, but it sure would have helped this time for the ladies to let Steph know how to drive through a miniature swamp like that! Morgaine at least should have said something she's not Navajo, but as usual she made some tired excuses and now we were stuck. Steph was looking pretty forlorn, and as she opened the driver door she stared down at the thick mud and hesitated. Morgaine was, as per usual, complaining, and

Robin just sat there. I was immediately irritated with everyone, jumped out and sank up to my calves in mud, great! We were well and truly stuck. Thankfully and miraculously, a truck came along just as we were inspecting the damage, and Steph jumped into the road to flag it down. After much talk about how not to drive on these roads (sigh), our erstwhile rescuer, who knew Robin, managed to rock the truck out of the mud. I was tired, irritable, and muddy, and insisted on driving, but at least everything was cool and we weren't stuck all night with Morgaine whining in my ear or anything. We were still a ways from home, and I'm sure Robin would have left us to go home to her kids, either walking or hitching a ride. It was extremely lucky someone came along considering how late it was. You rarely see another car on the rez but at least no one would drive past you and just leave you stranded.

The next morning Morgaine talked so much over breakfast that we were late getting out, and then Georgia stopped us again to talk, so we ended up being an hour late to meet the vet. I called him when we got to the diner and he came back out to meet us, and had a lot of interesting stuff to say about the condition of the Winslow tract and the cows grazing there. He told me that the Winslow ranch did not have enough grazing to support the head of cattle the BIA had put on it. He also thought the cows were suffering from malnutrition, and there was probably not enough water to sustain them either. Many of the calves that had been taken there or were born there were either dead or missing. It was hard to determine, as the area was so large and there was no other way to find the cows apart from on horseback. (Oh for my good riding days or an ATV!) I managed to persuade him to put his name on a report that said as much, and he reluctantly agreed. It wasn't as if there was any love lost between him and the BIA, it's just that the BIA was notorious for causing problems for people who opposed their decisions, and he didn't want to be seen as a troublemaker. The Dineh are extremely cautious about putting their name to anything or making any official statements. Understandable in that current removal climate, but it did make the work difficult if all you have to go on is "someone said."

After the meeting, Steph and I wearily headed off for the long drive home. Thankfully it was pretty uneventful, and after arriving home and having a long hot shower, I fell into my lovely bed and slept deeply.

XIII

August 7th, 1999

Muriel and I went up to Big Mountain in her beautiful big black truck to meet with some of the Dineh people and the vets at Winslow. Autumn, the drama queen that she is, had tried to do her chaos thing and re-arrange us. We did our best to ignore her and ended up without her tagging along, which was great because I found her incredibly annoying.

Muriel and I had a cool weekend; Morgaine couldn't come out to play, so David Oak said he would travel and translate for us. He took us over the mountain the "back way" in Muriel's truck, which meant driving where no vehicles normally go. It was a white-knuckle ride to say the least, there was no road most of the way, barely a dirt track. Sometimes we had to get out and rearrange rocks under the truck tires, half building a smoother track for the truck to travel over, gorgeous views, though. I wish I had the presence of mind to take more photographs, but cameras were a bit of a no-no on the rez. It reminded me of those cartoons you see where the cars are "walking" on their tires. We joked about Muriel being on her way to getting her "Indian driving license!"

On the way back home to LA we got stuck in the most horrendous traffic, so I put a call in to Ben to let him know we were safe. He was still talking about Autumn and how she was going to put together a hay run for the animals. Anything not to be outdone I guess! Many years later, Ben told me that he used to tell Autumn and me about what the other one did deliberately in some weird attempt at creating competition. What a ridiculous thing to do. Like I needed more motivation or the aggravation of someone doing that. It created so many more problems and stress.

XIV

Animal Abuse Report
August 1999

The Dineh people live under very aggressive livestock restrictions imposed by the Bureau of Indian Affairs. This is one form of harassment the BIA uses to try to force the Dineh to relocate from their homeland to the New Lands, so Peabody can have easy and unopposed access to one of the richest deposits of coal in North America. The "New Lands," located in Church Rock, New Mexico, were contaminated by a uranium spill and are toxic. The Church Rock spill is likely one of the worst single spills of radioactive waste in the U.S. The area is peppered by uranium mines, and on July 16, 1979 a dam burst sending eleven hundred tons of radioactive waste and ninety million gallons of contaminated liquid gushing into the surrounding land and waterways. The flood left residues of radioactive uranium, thorium, radium, polonium as well as traces of cadmium, aluminum, magnesium, manganese, molybdenum, nickel, selenium, sodium, vanadium, zinc, iron, lead and sulfates. The Rio Puerco River was also contaminated, which was used as a watering hole for the local Navajo livestock. In a report by the US Army Corps of Engineers it was said that if the dam had been built to legal specifications it might not have burst; a report supported by a "consensus" of engineers from the New Mexico State Engineers Office also came to the same conclusion. This is just another example of a mining company cutting corners, endangering the environment and the lives of both people and animals. The spill was never cleaned up appropriately, and a full investigation of how far the contamination had spread was never undertaken nor was support for those affected ever made available.

On Big Mountain, the Dineh have had about 90% of their animals reduced by confiscation. The BIA has a long history of animal abuse with the Dineh; the elder's recounted one incident when their livestock were rounded up, herded until they where exhausted and then burned alive, but of course there are no written reports of this.

One scheme cultivated by the BIA and the Navajo nation was to "allow" some of the Dineh's confiscated animals to graze on a piece of land called the Winslow Tract Ranch, near Leupp, Arizona. The ranch is managed by the Navajo/Hopi Land Commission, and purchased by the Navajo Nation specifically for grazing the Dineh's illegal livestock. "Illegal" livestock being the excess number of animals after the BIA had imposed number restrictions on the amount of animals each family were allowed to keep. The State Department of Agriculture holds sections of the ranch in trust, and the Navajo Nation owns the rest. The previous spring, the area had been declared a drought emergency and to date still had extremely poor grazing, and the only available water is salty. Our veterinary report states that approximately thirty to forty head of impounded cattle are very weak; their coats are rough, and the animals have body sores. It is the vet's professional opinion that these cows are reflecting their environment, i.e. lack of forage, heat extremes, salty water, and the distance they have to walk between forage and water. The BIA and the Navajo Nation remove animals from Big Mountain citing "overgrazing" and move the cattle to an area, which could hardly have recovered from a drought in one year. Makes perfect sense right?

There were numerous orphaned calves that show signs of malnutrition and lack of care. The calves' mothers' whereabouts were unknown. Some families had cattle missing. At the branding station I observed the cattle in poor physical condition. The land looked extremely sparse. The only available water was dirty, with dead frogs in it. No food, water, or shade was available to the cattle. One mother cow gave birth that day also without food, water, or shade. She had obviously been herded many miles. The cows were treated very roughly at the station. Previously an elder refused to brand one of her cows because it had a dislocated hip. The BIA took it and branded it anyway.

It was extremely difficult to find out what responsibilities the Navajo/Hopi Land Commission have with the cows at the Winslow Ranch. They won't share any information, or are deliberately vague. It is also hard to tell what responsibilities they informed the elders they expected from them at the time they confiscated their cattle. So far I have been unable to obtain anything in writing. It is extremely difficult for some of the people to get to Winslow to see their cows and take care of them. They had no transport, no money, and no trailers to take their horses so they could ride the range. The Navajo/Hopi Land Commission is often unwilling to cooperate in opening the gate when needed. For the elderly owners (over seventy years old) with no income, they also can't afford the four dollars per-head per-month grazing fee for the use of the range. Although the cattle were confiscated, the owners are still responsible for all fees or they will eventually lose the cattle. The ideal resolution was for the elders to be allowed to take their cattle home with them.

This is what they would like to do, but the BIA will not allow it, and would only impound the cows again.

It was the opinion of some of the families that their livestock was taken to Winslow to die, and their own people, the Navajo Nation, were not helping them at all, but are in fact, complicit in the deed. The situation was in desperate need of help with regular deliveries of feed and fresh water. Donations for veterinary costs, vehicles and gas, are also needed as are supporters who can coordinate trailers and horses for the elders to be able to care take of their own cows. About $10,000 annually was needed to make the grazing fee. This of course, is an impossible situation for everyone.

There is one case I specifically know of where one of the elder's horses was shot dead. The BIA has been known to do this if they cannot catch animals they wish to impound. The owners of the horse suspect the BIA was responsible for what happened. The modus operandi of the BIA is to arrive at the homes of the elders, armed and in force, generally in the middle of the night to induce as much stress and fear as possible. They then confiscate animals against the families' wishes, and have been known to attack elderly women and physically abuse them. The animals are treated roughly at the impoundment yards, and one horse was witnessed to have a gash in its head. There is rarely any food or water available for the animals. They are then sold at auction, with no compensation made to the owner. I doubt they end up anywhere good, more than likely at a slaughterhouse.

It seemed to me that the whole situation was set up to be lose/lose for the Dineh elders. An apparent scheme to allow the BIA and certain members of the Navajo Nation to legally take the Dineh's cattle, and everyone turns a blind eye because they want them off the land. The BIA make it absolutely impossible for the Dineh, and the reasoning behind the removal of the animals, that BM itself is becoming environmentally impacted by grazing cattle, seems absurd in the face of the condition of the land the cattle have been moved to. Eventually, the cattle are lost to the imposed red tape with no recourse for the owners. It is a hopeless situation. If you ever want to know what real corrupt bureaucracy is, try dealing with the BLM.

On the land itself, the sheep and cattle are constantly in danger of being poisoned by chemicals dumped from the mines that run into local creeks. One family had eighty-five sheep die in twenty-four hours after they drank poisoned water contaminated from the Peabody coalmine. There have been many other cases of poisoned animals since the mines opened, and there has never been any compensation paid to the families for this, their only livelihood.

The Relocation Act has been devastating to the Dineh. This has resulted in their livelihood being severely restricted, and as the people themselves do not have enough to eat, their domestic animals suffer from malnutrition, mange, ticks, fleas and flea anemia. They are unable to obtain veterinary help through lack of funds and transport in difficult terrain where weather conditions make roads impassable.

Stray dogs are mainly visible at the gas stations, begging for food. We have found them to be incredibly gentle and friendly. They suffer from malnutrition, mange, ticks, fleas and flea anemia. All of them are in extremely poor physical condition. On Hopi land, the veterinarians put microchips in all domestic dogs. If they pick up a stray with no microchip, they shoot the animal. Sheepdogs are generally in better shape, but also suffer from lack of food and have a hard life.

I have been told that currently there are some people picking up dogs on Big Mountain and either attempting amateur castration or some kind of ritual abuse. I saw one dog that had been missing from its owners, only to return with a raw penis and sores on the genital areas. These accusations are hard to prove, as there are no witnesses. The animals are rarely taken to the vets, as unfortunately, the closest vet is about two hours drive away, and the Dineh rarely have access to transport and certainly no money for food, let alone veterinarian costs. We help where we can.

Pregnancies in domestic animals generally go unchecked. This is due to not being able to reach a vet for spaying and neutering, as well as a lack of funding. That combined with a traditional belief system that allows animals to procreate at will, all fuel the suffering of cats and dogs. I know of fourteen puppies that have died through lack of care and starvation. I also know of two incidents where puppies were run over by people driving carelessly to a homestead and died because of their injuries. Neither of these incidents appeared to cause grief to the animal's owners, which is more than likely, the result of living through years of major stress, violence and abuse themselves, with no hope to cling to.

End of Report

On August 23rd I received an urgent communiqué from our on-site spokesperson for the Dineh. The message stated that the day before, the Hopi rangers had harassed one of the elders whilst she was trying to water her sheep. Grandma Rachel Silverbirch suffers from a heart condition and is over seventy years old. Previously whilst trying to stop the Hopi Rangers from impounding her animals she was physically attacked by them. Her medical record clearly states she had suffered physical injuries.

This Great Grandmother had lived on her land with her family her entire life; land that was now divided by a barbed wire fence. One side was Hopi Partition Land (HPL) and the other side Navajo Partition Land (NPL). Now, because of this fence, to get water for herself and her sheep she had to load up her truck with a barrel and drive down the mountain. The dirt roads to Grandpa and Grandma Silverbirch's homestead were some of the most difficult to drive on. In fact as young, able-bodied people we had been unable to reach her because adverse weather conditions had made the terrain too difficult for our vehicles to pass. Three million gallons of water is pumped right underneath her in the slurry line Peabody own, or rather, have stolen. Pristine drinking water from underground springs, which once fed many watering holes throughout the mesa, was now used to slurry coal. Yet when Grandma needed to water her sheep on Saturday with no water available, she opened the fence dividing the land and allowed her herd of one hundred sheep to drink from a puddle on the HPL side of the fence. She stood with the sheep, waiting to herd them back immediately after they had finished. Unfortunately, the Hopi Rangers saw her and told her to take her sheep back onto NPL and keep them there. They also told her that they would come back any time of day or night to watch her, and if she did it again they would confiscate all of her sheep. As you can imagine she is now very afraid, and we are extremely concerned about her health and safety. She has a permit from the Navajo Nation for all the sheep, but the Hopi Rangers do not recognize this permit. The Hopi Rangers have obviously singled her out for harassment. There is no way you could just happen to see Grandmother herding her sheep in this remote area unless you were following her around. On land where the homesteads are hundreds of miles apart, and the Hopi tribe lives far away, they would have to be sitting waiting at her fence line to watch for the Grandmother to make any kind of perceived infraction so they can harass her. This is nothing less than intimidation of a vulnerable elder and is disgusting behavior.

To immediately aid her plight we needed large plastic tanks for water, so that at least when she did go down the mountain she didn't have to do the trip many times. We also wanted supporters to live with her as long as possible to help her and her husband and be a witness to anything that happened. Disposable camera equipment was also needed to document the abuses.

XV

September 9th 1999

September was the month from hell: I lost my job, my prized laptop computer was stolen from work, and Simon English, one of my closest friends I had known from school, drowned. No one was ever sure if it was an accident or if he committed suicide. We still managed to collect an absolute ton of donations for the Dineh though. Star Trek producer Marty Hornstein and his friend Wayne, who had his own trucking company, kept us supplied with stake bed trucks and drivers to pick up donations in Malibu and Hollywood. We managed to fill a fifty-foot semi with all sorts of clothes, furniture, food, medical supplies and household supplies which was just incredible.

Fifteen cars traveled in the caravan that weekend. We all left LA at different times, partly because of necessity. No one could leave at the same time, and we also did not want to get spotted arriving on the mesa by the reservation police. Autumn took up a minibus full of people; Muriel and I loaded up her shiny black F150 and we took off about 12:30 pm. David, Drea and Renee were going to leave with us, but their car was late out of the shop, so we decided to head out without them. We were anxious to get going, Muriel is always anxious to get going!

We were on Highway 10 heading out of town when Ben called; apparently Autumn had left Susan and her friend behind because they had been late getting to her house. I guess he was hoping we would still be around to pick them up, but we were too far down the road to turn back. They ended up going with Ben, which really pissed him off as he was already overloaded and having mechanical issues. What a fun weekend this was going to be! In all, there were thirty-five of us including volunteers from three groups: the Social & Environmental Entrepreneurs (SEE) who was SDN's fiscal agent, the Action Resource Center (ARC), and people from United Spirits (a documentary and video library). Quite a few Dineh showed up to help as well.

Muriel and I had great conversations on the way, which included all the ridiculous questions we would ask the Dalai Lama if we ever were to meet him. "The Dal," as Muriel called him, was visiting LA at that time. We also tried to figure out what he would wear under his robes, reveling in our silly profanity. Of course, this was late in the day; we were getting quite ridiculous and quite stoned. Muriel was always a great driving companion. She was always organized with great food, and as her truck is a lot faster than mine we got up to Big Mountain in record time. We had both worked at good jobs, so we weren't short of a few dollars to make sure our ride was comfortable and had no issues. Sometimes, it was a hard strain to be the only one traveling who worked and had some spare cash. In our many journeys together, Ben and I could always rely on each other to have some emergency cash when no one else would have any.

As we were coming up on Flagstaff, the sky became the most incredible shade of indigo I have ever seen. The scenery was beautiful; the outline of the mesas was sketched in black in the fading twilight on the horizon. Dark trees lined our journey and stars began to flicker their light in the turning sky. Mother

Earth sure is a good artist. We had one narrow miss on the way up there; we had to brake hard from ninety mph to miss a couch that had suddenly appeared in the middle of the road. If we had swerved at that speed, we would have either hit oncoming traffic or turned the truck over. I looked around to see a semi and a panicked driver bearing down on us fast, so I just started shouting, "gas now!" and Muriel floored it so we didn't end up with a semi parked in our flat bed. It was a close call! The rest of the journey passed without significant incident, and we had a great drive.

Around midnight, Muriel and I crawled up Grandma Georgia's pitch-black dirt driveway. Autumn and her van load were already there. They had pitched some tents, so surprising Muriel and myself, I decided to crash in Autumn's huge tent, and Muriel, who refused the offer of sleeping surrounded by "nutters!" slept in her truck.

People had already started to rouse themselves when I woke up the next morning. Autumn's mum cooked us some eggs and bagels for breakfast, which was great. I had heard Ben and David's group arrive in the middle of the night. By the time I made it out of my sleeping bag, they had already taken off again to find David Garcia's Fox 11 TV crew, and Wayne's semi truck, which was supposed to be parked at Niyol Oaktree's house. They must have all slept fully clothed in their car seats, as by the time we woke up they were already waiting at the Chevron station and had, unfortunately, been spotted by the Hopi Rangers.

It was an awesome sight watching the semi haul up to Georgia's. I have no idea how they got that huge truck down the dirt road, which was extremely pitted, but thanks to the expertise of the driver and probably a lot of sweat, they did it. There was one part of the track that crosses a creek bed and it was usually quite difficult to get across even with our small trucks, let alone a semi. I was extremely impressed, and it was definitely a huge event for the Big Mountain people. The weather hadn't been bad lately, so the dirt road was fairly hard packed. If the weather had turned and started to rain, the semi truck would never have gotten down the road. The roads turn into quagmires of deep mud when the rain falls. We always would get stuck somewhere and have to drive really carefully, if not at all. Forget driving regular cars up there, as they just don't make it. Ben and Dave had shown the Fox 11 crew the way to Grandma Georgia's, so they had already set up and were busy filming the semi as it arrived. It was a tremendous sight. We had two news crews with us: Fox 11 from LA and CBS from Arizona who both aired our story on the 6 o'clock news that night.

After the grand entrance by Wayne, Marty, and the semi, we all gathered with the families who had heard the news we were coming. There were no telephones on the rez; so all news was spread by word of mouth. People rarely made the journey to visit each other; most of the homesteads had been abandoned as the people were moved on to the new lands under the Relocation Act. Everyone lived so far apart it made travel difficult, so we relied on Morgaine to visit each family with any news so they in turn could spread the word. To do this she would have to wait for Greystone to have a day off from work and find enough money for the gas it took to drive all over the rez. This sometimes took weeks, so it meant being well organized way ahead of time.

Before we unloaded the haul, some of the Dineh wanted to give speeches of thanks whilst Fox 11 filmed them. At one point, David Oak was speaking about the huge corporate takeover of their heritage and culture. He was getting extremely emotional, so Muriel decided to offer him a drink, as it was a hot day. The nearest beverage just happened to be a can of Coke, and she handed it to him on camera. To this day we find this so hilarious after we realized what she had done, handed him the number one product from the worlds largest evil corporation. Coca-Cola product placement couldn't have done it better! Even now I hear the words of the 1970s Coca-Cola song "I'd Like To Teach the World To Sing" every time I think of it. Morgaine made us all say something on camera, highly embarrassing indeed. I don't think I ever saw the footage. I hope at least my part is buried in an archive somewhere; never to see the light of day, although I would love to see Muriel's can of Coke episode again.

After a couple of hours of thanks and speeches, we started to unload the semi. Of course, the "Hollywood" people, who consisted of mainly men, filmed the unloading whilst the women did the lifting work. I always thought this a strange turn of role reversal, or is it? It always made me as mad as hell though watching healthy men stand around as my 110 pounds of nothing did all the lifting and carrying. Sometimes, as I was unloading trucks, some guy who was trying to chat me up would stand by the truck, cracking jokes, hoping to impress me, when all the time I would have been more impressed if they had helped me carry shit!!!!!

Before we could organize a proper distribution of the semi's contents, people started flocking in like birds and taking stuff away. Morgaine was frantic as her precious office equipment we had painstakingly collected was being loaded onto other people's trucks and hauled off. I asked Muriel to bring her truck up, and we loaded it with the furniture and other items we had brought up specifically for the SDN office. One of the items was an amazing rug that my girlfriend Debra had donated, which was previously used on a film set she had worked on. It was, as always, quite comically unorganized and chaotic. Autumn directed Muriel to the wrong storage place. I guess she hadn't known we had planned to store Morgaine's office equipment in Georgia's shed, but it was another example of how she would always interfere, and instead of consulting would make a decision that was misinformed, creating more work for everyone. So for a few hours we had to reload it all again onto the truck and bring it back to the shed whilst Vic, his son and their friends worked on rebuilding the office.

As our organization grew larger and our donations became bigger, the integrity of the relationships within Gaia Communications started to deteriorate. There just didn't seem to be anything we could do to stop it. Anger and frustrations quickly boiled to the surface like soup left on the stove too long. Obsessions lay ungratified and emotions turned raw. It was as if a bad energy had seeded inside all of us and would not let go, but kept on growing like an unwanted weed. Perhaps it was the "amplifier energy" that seemed to hang over the mountain like a cloud of doom. That weekend in particular seemed to become a turning point as relationships fractured under the surface. As it turned out, it wouldn't be the same again for quite some time. I think what was partly to blame was our sheer exhaustion, and no matter how hard we tried to organize and help, the Dineh's situation was just too dysfunctional. It was like we kept throwing things into the big black hole of Big Mountain, and nothing stuck and nothing seemed to make a difference to the big picture. Oh sure, we won many battles and had many good things happen, but the wheel turns extremely slowly. There was so much despair, with no hope for the future. There was a huge amount of need, and our limited resources just didn't cut it. This was in the "dark" days before social media had taken over. I can't imagine how different things would have been if we'd had access to such an amazing tool. The internet and popular computer use were still in their infancy stages, and Ben and I were one of very few that even owned computers. The elders had not stopped fighting, but the next generation was scattered and broken. Once the elders went, unless some amazing spirit came through, it started to feel like the cause would be lost. After all, Peabody just had to wait out a few more years until the elders died, and then there would be nothing to stop them unless the next generation really pulled it together.

After the morning's toil was done, Muriel and I loaded up the few bags of food that were left, and, along with Steve and Laura from SEE, tagged along with Ben and the TV crews to deliver supplies to the families they had planned on interviewing. Muriel was getting a little annoyed as she didn't want to haul ass on the washboard dirt roads to catch up with Ben, who of course wouldn't slow down too much for us as it would hold everyone up. I don't blame her; after every visit my truck ended up in the shop with one thing or another burned out. The roads were extremely tough on the vehicles, so if you didn't want to park your truck at the garage on your return, you drove a bit more carefully.

First we went to Mary Black's home to interview and film her with all of the rugs she had woven from her sheep's wool. She didn't speak any English, but stared at us with her sharp, black eyes and spoke quietly in Dineh. As I leaned against the truck waiting, I watched the Grandmother run her keen eyes over everyone and observe everything closely; they never seemed to miss anything. Her people's words of respect for the Earth were always punctuated with the loss they felt for their way of life, devastation caused by the government demands on their ancient homelands, physical and mental abuse from the BIA, ill health from the coalmines, alcohol addiction taking their men and splitting their families, poverty and starvation. Their pleas to the powers that be always seem to go unheeded, promises were made and broken again, a vicious cycle that started more than a hundred years ago. Our help seemed to fill a tiny part of the black hole of devastation they were in, or at least get them through a few months. Usually it felt as if I got more from the giving than they did being the recipient. Often, people would ask me why I did what I did, and I always responded the same way. Because I got so much more out of it than any money I spent, or anything I ever gave. Their situation and that of the Earth broke my heart over and over again.

As the sun began its journey back to the other side of the world, its fading light casting awe inspiring hues of red and purple across the vast sky, we headed back to base camp at Grandma Georgia Pine's. We didn't expect Autumn and her mum back until late. They had gone to Coal Mine Mesa and Star Mountain, which was a long, hard drive, so we set up the potluck and ate.

Ben got hauled off for a four-hour talk with Georgia and Sally in their house. I felt slightly left out and had to wonder why as a main organizer for Gaia Communication I was not included. It felt slightly disrespectful, elitist, and I didn't like all the secrecy. "Oh well," I thought, "bugger them, I'll enjoy myself here." It was probably the largest camp-out we had ever had up there, including Vic, his son and his friend, who were rebuilding the office; Sun, Susan, and some other young activists from the Action Resource Center house in Venice. As I was handing out the food, I noticed Sun just sitting there staring at his plate. I asked him what was wrong and assured him it was all vegetarian. Well, it wasn't the food that was wrong it was the plate. It was paper and probably made from some ancient forest somewhere. I hadn't really thought about that aspect. All this time working hard for the Dineh, respecting animals enough not to eat them, I hadn't thought of where the paper plates came from that I had been buying regularly to bring up for camp. I apologized and stupidly offered a plastic camping plate, but that wasn't going to solve the issue - plastic was just as bad if not worse than paper! The production of plastic polluted the Earth with vile toxins and hurt those who lived in the area of the factories. I am always amazed at how much I have yet to learn, and thereafter always packed reusable plates and cutlery.

Our eclectic group hung out around the fire eating, laughing, and telling stories until it was time to hit the sack. Ben returned, tired from his long meeting, and refused to share what it had all been about, which made my feelings worse. Our friendship had started to disintegrate, and every time he shut me out of meetings I got more and more pissed off and resentful.

That night it started to rain torrents. An incredible lightning and thunderstorm came up which you could hear traveling closer and closer across the vast mesa. It sounded like the Thunder Beings were bowling with mountain boulders, and the lightning was so bright you couldn't keep your eyes open to look at it. Autumn and Elena came back late with an abandoned puppy. The poor thing had irritated skin, was riddled with fleas and couldn't stop chewing on himself. Mindless of the fleas, Muriel and I kept him in our tent and let him snuggle between our sleeping bags. He was so good he even told us when he needed to go out and pee. He didn't seem to mind the rain at all. Muriel and I watched him from the tent opening, hoping he wouldn't run away in the rain - then we'd have to get soaked running after him. But nope, this little pup knew where his bread was buttered, and came trotting back to get well loved and dried in our snug tent. We took the puppy back to LA with us, and Muriel looked after him until a kind lady adopted him and called him Rez. He lived a long and extremely good life. What a blessing; he was one of the very few lucky ones.

Amazingly enough my small tent held up throughout the torrential rainstorm. It was quite cozy actually. No one got washed out or hit by lightning, and we woke to an extremely beautiful day: clear skies, fresh air, and sunshine. We put together our favorite breakfast of bagels, coffee and cigarettes and started to pack for the long journey home.

It took us a while to actually leave the mountain, which always seemed to be the case. Autumn, Elena, Susan and company went off with Fox 11 to see the petroglyphs. Stress was still very visible as the negative energy seeped into our pores. We were all having a hard time dealing with each other's personality quirks after working so hard and long on such a tough campaign. People had started to show what I would now call "issue trauma" from years spent driving the twelve hours up to the rez either every weekend or every other weekend, collecting donations, trying to get an uncaring population to pay attention, working a fulltime job, and then there was the media blackout to contend with. We were basically burned out but didn't recognize it.

Morgaine, as usual, couldn't stop talking and as soon as she found out Fox 11 had gone to the petroglyphs without a

Dineh guide she went ballistic. Not that it would have worked because the guide would need a ride, and then someone would have to bring them all the way back to Big Mountain, delaying our departure for hours. That didn't mean much to Morgaine, but it meant utter exhaustion or being delayed by another night, which was a lot to the people that had come up from LA. The petroglyphs were on the way out, and Ben and I had visited the location many times without a guide. The cliffs they were drawn on were set back from the road, but you had to drive over some rough terrain to actually see them. It's an eerily quiet place where you can just feel the ancient spirits lingering. I'm not sure if anyone has done a proper study of the place, but it always felt magical to me. The air seemed thicker there, heavier, or just more intense. Every time we visited there seemed to be a lone owl waiting and watching from one of the high crevices, which lent itself even more to the eerie atmosphere. In Native American lore, owls can sometimes have a negative connotation, signifying death or a bad omen. For me, no animal or bird could ever symbolize anything negative, and I always sought their magical aspect. They were the silent sentinels: full of wisdom, watching, waiting and somehow otherworldly.

Muriel and I took the opportunity of Morgaine's attention being diverted to haul ass out of there. We hitched the borrowed generator to the back of the truck and hit the road. Autumn took the ARC and SEE people back to LA in the rental van. David and Drea went with them, since they wanted to stop and see the rock art on the way out as well. Ben went on to visit his new home in Colorado, and Vic and his son left later, getting stuck on the way back with a broken-down car. On the way home, I called Nick and Adam, two friends who lived in North Hollywood, to see if they could meet us at Marty's to help unload the generator. Luckily, they were available and really cool about it because there was no way Muriel and I could unload it by ourselves, and Marty was not in the best of health, so he couldn't really help either. It was one of those occasions where you just keep putting one step in front of the other and believing that it would all work out in the end. When we arrived at Marty's in Sherman Oaks, the guys came over and helped us lift the generator out of Muriel's truck, which was no easy task. Finally, I got home around 10:30 pm, had a quick shower to get rid of the weekend's dirt, dust, and mayhem, and fell into bed. Muriel took the little flea-ridden puppy and cared for him until his new permanent home was found.

XVI

October 22nd 1999

After much planning for this caravan and a helluva few months for me, we again took off for BM. This caravan consisted of Muriel and me in my small Ford truck, and Vic in his truck. It was one of our smaller missions, with only a few people. We left LA about 12:30 pm after packing the truck to the hilt with clothes, food and some medical supplies. Vic was taking up a bunch of food and had left earlier in the day. It was a pretty uneventful drive; unfortunately it was getting rather boring for me now. I missed driving with Ben; we always somehow had such an adventure. Muriel was a very cool companion and great fun to be with, but with Ben there was always an air of dangerous adventure and the unexpected happening. He always managed to push the envelope and get me to do things I would never have done, and still wouldn't do, without him, and things always seemed to happen around him. There always seemed to be the element of magic around when Ben and I traveled, as we were both spiritual and employed various ritualistic protection techniques to help our missions. Muriel wasn't into the esoteric, so that element was missing. With Ben, I could always say when I spotted Magda and Dagda, my two "medicine" crows that travel with me. With Muriel, although she would understand, she wouldn't really be into it, so I never bothered, just silently acknowledged their presence and help.

We arrived at Morgaine's trailer around midnight Big Mountain time. Vic was already there, looking like the wild wolf he was. Morgaine was always pleased to see us, and it was also nice to get such a great welcome after the long drive. We all decided to camp down for the night in the trailer as the office was out of order, the boards on the windows had been taken off, so it wasn't suitable to sleep in. Muriel was not at all happy with the arrangement, preferring more privacy, but BM was what it was, always unpredictable and privacy was scarce. Morgaine and I shared her bed and settled to gossip about what had been going on with Greystone. She had fallen very much in love with him, and it would appear he had some ardent feelings for her too, but it all had to be kept a big secret as he was married with children. I don't care one way or another what people got up to and could hardly set myself up as a judge of character, having had such a hedonistic past myself, but it just didn't feel that this was going to go anywhere good. I wanted to believe it would all work out for everyone, and it was part of the Dineh culture for a man to be allowed more than one wife. The guys always love the idea, but does it truly ever work out? It doesn't appear to. Perhaps in the past, when there was a lot of manual work to be done around growing and preparing food, it would have been a must to have more than one woman taking care of the food production. There would have been an entirely different attitude involved, as the patriarchal mindset of pitting woman against woman and having power over them all wouldn't be there. I never understood it all though, and am as much in favor of having a multitude of husbands to do all the work as I am in having a multitude of wives. Thinking about it though, are a multitude of husbands any good? I mean how you could put up with more than ONE man's crap, for gawd's sake!

It was very late when we finally got to sleep, or rather when Morgaine let me go to sleep. Bless her cotton socks, but she never stopped talking! We wanted to get up early the next day, but as usual that didn't turn out to be the case. In the morning, we loaded up the truck as quickly as we could, and all set off for David Oak's to deliver dog food and ask someone to translate for us for the tour around the mountain.

Morgaine and Vic then went off to the Chevron station to meet a lawyer Vic had arranged to come out to the land and help with the legal issues of the Relocation Act. David came with Muriel and I to translate, and the three of us took off on the back route to Rachel and James Silverbirch's home, which was as yet unexplored by us. We had wanted to map out the route for a long time in case we needed it in the future to avoid the Feds, so Muriel was put in charge of navigation and map making. I drove, and much to his enormous pleasure and our discomfort, David Oak was squeezed in the middle of us two white, blonde bahannas, God knows how in that tiny truck. People always used to quip about my Ford truck and the same old joke about what Ford stood for (found on road dead), but man that was the little truck that could. It was a beautiful drive across the flat plains of the mesa, and the day was equally gorgeous. Totally clear blue azure skies, sunshine, and a light breeze; we couldn't have asked for a better day.

We headed for Blue Canyon, a deep ravine of the most spectacular rock formations. David said that the rocks were ancient people who had been turned to stone and now stood around as sentinels. They sure did look like it. Tall sandstone pinnacles with grooved faces cut out by the elements. They appeared like mystical, silent, and eerie watchers of the world, guarding ancient secrets. As the road grew narrow, steeper and rocky, I became increasingly worried. The food load we were hauling was very heavy in the back of my little truck. It was only a two-seater, so David had to sit in the middle and, unfortunately for me, inhibited my driving with his huge belly. I was getting concerned that if the truck slipped out of control I wouldn't be able to handle it properly because David's girth would not let me maneuver the steering wheel, and before you knew it we would be off the edge of the ravine! I surely don't know how someone with not a lot of food available gets such a large stomach!

Just at the moment I was starting to have my inner meltdown, David's arms started to creep around the back of my seat and drop onto my shoulder, and then his fingers began to twirl around on my skin, which was most disconcerting. I was concentrating so hard on keeping us on the road and not pitching us into the ravine this was the last thing I needed. He's definitely a fairly harmless flirtatious type, but this was getting worse by the second for me. I was trying to figure out how to tactfully disengage in those close, cramped quarters as the truck struggled to get us up a really steep hill.

Being so distracted, I wasn't watching out for the engine over-heating, which I should have been on such a steep hill and with so much weight in the back. I decided to pull over at the top of the hill to rest the car and extract myself from David, but as we crested the hill, water and steam started to piss out of the radiator. The truck had overheated, and I had been too busy trying to figure out how to get away from David to notice. I stopped and jumped out extremely annoyed with David, and with myself for getting so distracted and not keeping an eye on the truck. The radiator water was flooding out and there was nothing else for it but to wait for it to cool down. When we opened up the bonnet to try and figure it out, no problem was apparent. We filled up the radiator with more water, but that just came pissing straight out again. David, who we finally figured out, had been drinking heavily the night before, started vomiting fabulously under a tree. As is often the case out there, things had gone from bad to worse in seconds, and I was furious.

The sun was hot, but at least we were still in daylight with plenty of time left before dark. We waited a while, but there was really only one thing left to do, and that was to walk the rest of the way and get help. It was perhaps five more miles to their homestead, and it wasn't going to be a pleasant walk in the heat. Luckily, we had plenty of water and supplies. David was standing around contemplating something, and he suddenly held up his index finger and said,
"It's at times like this we need a wish." It was a short, fat finger, and I don't know, he either blew on it or kissed it or licked it and then held in the breeze. Muriel and I remained totally unimpressed.

I walked to the back of the truck to change into my boots for the hike, and just as we were reluctantly packing up, wouldn't you know it, the wish came true. Grandpa James and Grandma Rachel Silverbirch came driving down the dirt road in their big ol' white truck like the saviors they were. We were all incredibly relieved and happy. It would have been a long hot walk, with no way of knowing if the old couple was at home or not. The walkie-talkies didn't work at that distance, and our cell phones had no signal up there. In true BM style, it could easily have turned into a complete nightmare and a whole week of being stuck. I was much relieved; even though the truck was still broken this at least meant we could get to a working phone and call Vic and Morgaine. And it meant that if we did get stuck, Grandpa and Grandma were at least at home to host us.

After some discussion, the decision was made to go to the store and get some radiator sealant. Muriel and I unloaded some food into the back of the Silverbirches' truck and jumped in the truck bed to go with them. David decided to stay with my truck and wait for us to come back to pick him up. I don't think he felt too well so he was probably going to catch some shut-eye under a tree. The elders were on their way to check out a livestock sale. It made me really sad to think they had to sell some of their sheep, and at the pathetic price they were asking of six to twenty dollars a head - that's the price of a sheep's life! Unbelievable.

I called Morgaine from the store; luckily she had her radiophone with her. I told her to come and get us by nightfall if we hadn't made it back by then and she said they would. Well at first Vic said "maybe", but I was in no mood for jokes. It had been a long, hot and exhausting not to mention irritating morning! In retrospect, I should have told them that if we had not made it back by the next day to come and get us then.

I enjoyed the ride back up the mountain with the Silverbirches, two of my favorite elders. It was mid afternoon and the weather was beautiful. The sky was scattered with wonderful fluffy clouds that seem to continuously morph into mythical creatures. I tried to take note of the route, but we went two different ways, and the landscape just looked the same to me. Our running joke about Indian directions always went something like "turn right at the second grey rock next to the tree that flowers in winter!" This of course worked very well if you had lived on the same land since you were born, but for city girls it was just bemusing.

When we returned to my truck, we filled up the radiator with sealant and water and then I drove it, limping back to their homestead. Muriel and I chatted with their son, Jerry who spoke some English, and then Grandpa James got on with fixing the truck. Grandpa sure did laugh at us. Everything we did seemed to be funny to him. I looked around to see where David had gotten to and saw him walking into a shed, obviously to crash out again. He paused at the doorway and beckoned me to follow. I couldn't believe it, what the hell was the man thinking! Wild horses wouldn't drag me in there, but of course Grandpa saw him and just gave me that Dineh disapproving look. There was no way to explain to Grandpa that there was nothing between us, and I wouldn't even be with David if hell froze over, so I just sat down in the dirt where I was. It was really aggravating of David to have done that, and so disrespectful. I preferred to watch Grandpa James repair the truck and silently fumed over David, whom I blamed for getting us into this mess in the first place. It never seemed to matter that I couldn't communicate with the elders in the same language; they had a way of being that was very comfortable just to be with.

As Grandpa worked on the truck, their herd of sheep and goats came wandering back by themselves from their daily foraging. The goats and sheep were so different in nature. Goats get into everything, and these were curiously sniffing around what we were doing; they were so friendly you could pet them. The sheep on the other hand, just ran away from you, even if you aren't actually heading towards them. I kept trying to get close to them, but it was impossible and hilarious. I decided then that I preferred goats. Amazingly enough, it didn't take long for Grandpa to repair the radiator and get it back in the truck. I still wasn't quite sure what happened. The metal clips holding the radiator in seemed to have just burst open. Probably all that weird David energy!

Grandpa even came up with the perfect screws to attach the fan cover as well. I was so impressed. It was marvelous, and I was much relieved. Grandma Rachel didn't seem very well at all. I think she was upset about the BIA coming around for the sheep and freaking everybody out, and she had heart problems in the past. The sheep and goats had been impounded by the BIA and treated so roughly some were injured. All the sheep seemed ok though; only one was still limping a bit. The Grandmas are especially extremely attached to their animals. All of the sheep and goats have a name of sorts. The Dineh never really give one name like 'Mabel,' it would be more like, 'The one that was born in the spring of the dropping tree that had a difficult birth.' Even though they killed them for food, the affection and concern they felt for the animals seemed no less. From my experience, the elders always treated their animals with respect and affection. I could never agree with eating meat under any circumstances, but at least here they were treated well, allowed to roam freely and behave in their animal nature. And there was no hope in hell of persuading any Dineh elders to become vegetarian any time soon.

It was weird how much the BIA picked on Rachel and James. I wonder if it was the particular area they lived in, which was more remote than others, or some other reason. It was difficult to get much information out of their son, Jerry, about anything. His English was good, but you have to say things in such a specific Dineh way to get the answer you're looking for. Our thought processes, the way we describe things and how we think, are so completely different you have to kind of get into the Dineh frame of mind to communicate effectively. We spent some time talking, and he showed me his horses. One of the horses just wandered around following Grandpa, even poking his head into the hogan when Grandpa went inside which was hilarious. Jerry was obviously very proud of them, and they were really lovely animals. Rachel kept her eye on us though. It made me laugh, but it was also a little disconcerting that the white female supporters have earned such a reputation around here more's the pity.

We waited for Morgaine and Vic, but when they hadn't turned up by about 8pm we decided to get back to Big Mountain ourselves, as the truck seemed ok. I insisted on using the main road, which was the long way round, even though David didn't want to. I sure as hell wasn't going to risk losing the truck again and getting stranded in the dark across open country, so we took the road. His faith in driving cross country in the dark, steep ravines on narrow dirt tracks in a truck that didn't make it the first time was not something I was going to agree to just because it was going to take us an extra hour to get back. At least, if we broke down on the main road, there was a good chance of someone coming along. If we broke down again cross-country there was fat chance of anyone driving along to help. Dineh or no, I didn't care much for David's survival skills - especially on a hangover. When we stopped for gas Muriel found a kitten stranded by the dumpster, so we took it with us. It was a real cute marmalade about ten weeks old and full of fleas.

When we finally got back to the trailer, we found out that Morgaine, Vic and Bonnie had come to rescue us, and had their own adventure, if you can call it that. Vic's truck had got stuck in the sand, and they had spent two hours trying to dig themselves out. Vic was furious with Morgaine who, as I've said, is of no help in these situations, apart from stressing everyone out even more. Eventually, some guy who was walking to his neighbor's house found them and got some help. Amazing for them they were so lucky, but I guess that's how things happened on the rez.

Vic's grey hair looked utterly wild when he walked in - as if he had stuck his hand in an electric socket and to say he was less than happy was a gross understatement; he was fit to be tied. What a night it was for everyone! Muriel got really grumpy again because she had to bed down in the trailer with all of us smelly lot and the flea-ridden kitten. Morgaine was not happy about having the kitten in the trailer, but we steadfastly refused to put it outside. It was too late to set up the truck to sleep in or pitch a tent, so we just had to find a spot to crash out on and be happy about it. I was too used to sleeping with a bunch of smelly, snoring people in hogans and teepees, so as long as I was warm and safe I couldn't care less.

We got up late again the next day and Morgaine cooked us eggs for breakfast. After eating and listening to more of her talking, we headed out of the trailer to check on the work that had been done on the office. I couldn't believe what a mess they had made of the floor. I don't know what Morgaine and Greystone were thinking in redoing the floor; it just created a huge amount of work and delayed the use of the office even more. We talked some more and then left to take Rebecca home and get a good start on the day. Luckily, Rebecca's kids wanted the kitten. There were plenty of playmates for it, as Rebecca is the local animal person. That was a hard decision, but I felt stupid bringing another stray kitten back to LA, and Muriel was allergic to cats. That was another decision I came to regret later and I wouldn't burden them like that again, but at the time I thought it was the best solution. I promised to make sure she got plenty of cat and dog food for all of her animals the next time we came up, and thereafter always came with huge bags of food for the cats and dogs. When we stopped at the gas station, we ended up helping a couple of guys who had broken down, which is a very regular thing on the rez. Funnily enough, they were on their way to David Oak's house - probably to smoke some and get drunk.

The ride home was a long and slow one. We had to stop and top up the water in the radiator as we still had a slow leak, and I was especially paranoid about it and so wouldn't drive very fast, much to Muriel's annoyance. I definitely didn't want to get stuck again, and once I get an idea into my head that I want to be home nothing is going to stop me. Man what a weekend, I had BM lag for a few days after that one!

XVII

Christmas Run of 1999

The Caravan Diaries

A poem from Erica Hamilton to Summer, Christmas 99

"Here's a little ditty I wrote a while back, it makes me think of you." Erica Hamilton

STARE IT DOWN
When the danger comes
to close your eyes
When doubt creeps into sleep
When stomp turns into cautious steps
and the challenge just seems too steep

Stare it down
Stare it down

The time has come to
STARE IT DOWN

You must wear your passion
like a warrior, girl
cuz the path you took ain't paved
Nothing you get will be given
and everything you've lost must be saved

We had two trailers parked in a North Hollywood film storage lot, which had been donated to us to store the increasing supply of donations coming in for the Dineh that Christmas. It was great to have these as none of us had a storage space where we could keep all the large items we were given.

By Tuesday, the blue trailer was packed with thirteen boxes of various canned and dried food; one box of books and clothes, one box of shoes, three bags of groceries, two 25lbs bags of flour, 25lb sugar, 16lb of cat food, 50lb of dog food, four rolls of material, six bags of clothes, two pairs of sneakers and one large cushion. The white trailer contained nine palates of Ocean Spray juice, two palates of toys and ten bags of clothes.

I was extremely skeptical about the donation of juice that Autumn and her mother had organized. Nine palates is an extraordinary amount of juice all packed in small plastic bottles. I just saw a ton of plastic waste that had nowhere to go on the rez, but Autumn hadn't thought beyond feeling proud of her own accomplishments and her desperate need for praise. There is such a thing as giving and making things worse than they were, and I thought the nine palates of juice were just that. More juice than anyone could drink, and even more toxic waste to sit around trashing the ground. I mean who was going to go around the rez and haul away all that plastic? There are no recycling programs on the rez!

Stefan, who worked at the Santa Monica farmers market, wrangled the following donation: one crate of cabbage, one crate of broccoli, one crate of corn, six boxes of apples, four boxes of potatoes, one box of pasta, one crate of carrots, six 10lb bags of oranges, and one box of clothes. This was such a fantastic donation of fresh vegetables, which are extremely rare and hard to get on the rez. There were also various donations from other sources too numerous to mention.

Wayne Nelson left LA in his semi truck Friday morning. It was packed to the brim with donations of bedroom furniture, toys, food, clothes and blankets. All collected from many people including David and Drea Crouch. Star Trek producer, Marty Hornstein drove with Wayne to keep him company.

My small caravan included Christine Grey and I in my truck. Christine was a single mother who had found out about our mission from a friend and felt called to help. Erica Hamilton, an environmental and animal rights activist from LA drove with Stefan in his jeep. We left LA around 3pm Friday afternoon, and immediately hit awful traffic until we were well onto the I-15.

Stefan and Erica had a hell of a journey with no heat and a ragtop roof on the jeep. I had looked at the truck before we left and told him I thought it would be a tough, cold ride, but he was determined to ride up. True Big Mountain troopers. We ended up stopping at Denny's in Flagstaff because the poor things were so cold and were having such a rough ride they needed a break. Christine offered to switch places with Erica for the remaining journey. We finally made it to Black Mesa at 6 am LA time and had an hours catnap in the trucks before turning around to go meet Wayne, Marty and the semi from the Chevron station to guide them in.

As we were driving past the mine entrance on the tarmac road to meet the semi, Wayne sailed past us going the other direction, heading towards the mesa. I guess they had decided to go it alone! We tried to wave him down, but he didn't see us, so we ended up spinning around and chasing him down. That was funny! Ever tried to catch a semi going full steam ahead? It truly is a beautiful sight to see a semi packed full of goodies taking those dirt roads. Lucky for us we had wonderful weather, thanks to the Goddess, who kept it bright and clear but just a little crisp.

We spent a good part of the morning unloading at Georgia Pine's as the kids ripped into all the toys. We loaded up Rachel Aspen's car and Jane and Esther Sycamores' truck a couple of times with some great stuff for Christmas. That too was a great sight to see: a hefty donation going to the families. So often we had wished we had more to give away. Wayne and the boys did a great job, a man with a heart big enough to match his girth!

Wayne and Marty turned around and drove straight back to LA, as they had to get the semi back for Sunday morning. Exhausted but happy, we spent the rest of the day organizing those thousands of bottles of juice and setting up some furniture in the office while Greystone and Rebecca finished the floor. Sara came by with the Sycamore sisters; it was good to see that beautiful young one. A couple of years later Sara ran away from the rez, and every so often the Grandmothers would ask me to find her, which I did, but the girl didn't want to go back. She hated the rez because of all the abuses she had suffered and was struggling to come to terms with in her life. I wonder what she is doing now, and I hope she found some peace somewhere.

We set up our bedding to crash in the office, ate some of the veggie stew I'd made at home, stoked the fire, and settled in for the night. Morgaine, as usual, talked my ear off for ages whilst the rest of the gang snored in dreamy mountain heaven.

It was a bit of a cold night, and it wasn't too easy to sleep or get up and keep the fire going, but we were happy enough. In retrospect, I wish we had gone to stay in Georgia's hogan, but that was before I knew the political consequences of Morgaine insisting we stay with her instead of with Georgia. What I didn't realize was that Morgaine was insisting we stay with her for a reason, or that Georgia might feel concerned that we weren't staying with her because of Morgaine's situation. Apparently, Morgaine's love affair with Georgia's son had started to unravel the good relationships between the two. Plus the hogans are so cozy; they have had so many ceremonies in them that the atmosphere is rich with good energy and I usually have really interesting dreams.

I was determined to get up early and head out to Coal Mine Mesa to deliver supplies, but when I woke to one of Georgia's supporters, Toby, drumming a morning Buddhist prayer, I felt incredibly reluctant to leave my warm sleeping bag. Toby was one of the volunteers organized by Flagstaff Big Mountain Support Group who stayed at Georgia's homestead to help out with the sheep and other work. Morgaine rustled up some breakfast for us, and as soon as I could motivate everyone, we headed out, first stopping at Georgia's, as we hadn't yet visited her. We couldn't actually help but stop since Georgia must have heard us driving past and came out to beckon us in. I didn't like the look of it, but when a Grandma tells you to do something you do it. Something was going on and I was about to find out what it was.

Unfortunately, it turned out to be a very bad idea as we ran into the full-on soap opera of the Morgaine and Pine family drama. All four of us - Stefan, Christina, Erica and I - were propped up on the couch like naughty school kids. I thanked

Georgia for all her hospitality over the years, and told her that this was the last official Gaia caravan run for a while as we were having a hard job finding help in LA anymore. Ben was moving his family to Colorado and had decided to focus more of his attention and funds on making sure his family was secure. They had given so much to the cause and living in a tiny-converted garage in LA. There is only so much you can do when you have your own kids, and for my part I was just purely exhausted and burned out.

Georgia's two daughters, Sally and Irene, started telling me in a none too polite way that they didn't want Morgaine there anymore and they had chosen someone else to work with them. I looked at them, astonished, as this was the first I was encountering such hostility from them. They continued to demand computer equipment and solar power; since this was also asked none too politely my response was,

"Oh …ok good luck with that…. hope you're not looking at me, kids!" Irene continued on in a very aggressive tone that she and her mother wanted to see the SDN fiscal records, as they had heard that people in LA were making a bunch of money and they weren't seeing any of it!! I had to stop myself from laughing at this point, so I just said,

"There is no money, but I will ask Gary Sweet to send the report to you. It shouldn't be too much of a problem as it is nearly tax time and he would be doing it anyway."

I kept glancing at Georgia and wondering if she was really aware of what her daughters were saying, but there was really no mistaking their attitude. I was getting a little annoyed with them and continued,

"Then you can see that there is no money, and nobody was renting any limousines and drinking martinis on the Dineh funds." Irene said that people must be getting something out of it or why would they do it? I was aghast, I had spent thousands of dollars of my own money donating to the Dineh, spent most of my spare time helping them, and now I was facing this juvenile inquisition from women with an agenda. I endeavored to remain calm and answered,

"I cannot speak for anybody else, but I do it for spiritual reasons." She didn't look happy at that and replied

"I don't believe that people do it for those reasons; they must get something out of it." What a utter dichotomy to find oneself in, facing a Dineh person who was supposedly more in touch with the land and Spirit than I, but was making such a shallow statement! Was it because I was white that she couldn't believe I was getting no financial gain out of this, or was it because she wouldn't do anything without some personal gain?

Obviously this was an extremely uncomfortable situation for us to find ourselves in especially for Erica, Stefan and Christina. I wondered if it was giving them doubts as to our organizations integrity, which would hurt us immensely. I continued to explain and said that, for me, it was not just about the Dineh or their culture; that I and Gaia Communications were predominantly environmentalists, and our work here was about helping the people who were resisting coal mining and trying to protect the Mother Earth. I told her that it didn't matter to me whether it was the Dineh or other people who were here, that I was here solely for the Earth and nothing and nobody else. Well that didn't go down well either, so she told me to send the report to Lisa Pine. I was horrified. I wasn't about to get any financial report and send it to Lisa. The only thing I had heard about Lisa from her own brother - was how much she had stolen from the SDN and taken off with some boyfriend to spend the money on booze, so that was the end of that request.

The whole situation was a great shame. I used to like Sally, and I had a lot of respect for Georgia, but I no longer felt comfortable there. I don't think that the sisters were interpreting things they said properly to Georgia, or the things we said. Georgia was sweet and thanked me when we left. It was as if she was pointedly doing that to somehow let me know she was grateful for all of our efforts in a subtle way. I felt she was in a hard place, stuck between having firsthand knowledge of our work for years, and not understanding properly how negative her daughters were being to us. I know it was also hard for them to trust; most white people only wanted to know them to take advantage in some way. It is hard to think it is not criminal to take advantage of people who are already in the worst place possible. Well, officially it might be criminal, but as 'officials' commit most of the crimes against the Dineh, I guess no one cares. Being forced to face the third degree and questioning my ethics in front of new supporters disturbed me very much. This could have been incredibly bad for our organization. Amazingly enough, the crew saw the negative energy being directed at me and was incredibly supportive. I was extremely grateful to them for this; otherwise it would have made the whole trip disastrous.

Years later I heard that Georgia still asked after us and why we no longer came. She called us, "the people who had brought up the big trucks." It affirmed in my mind that she was unaware of what her daughters had said and its consequences. Unfortunately, this has been somewhat of a problem for supporters in the past. Locals have directed negative energy at them, and they have felt so unwelcome that they have left, never to return.

It is hard to cast blame, as the Dineh have been through so much. Betrayal and hopelessness is a bitter circle all too easily played out on the rez.

So after all that, we trucked off and had a pleasant easy drive across Big Mountain to Coal Mine Mesa. We dropped in on Grandpa and Grandma Alder first, and I was delighted to see their hogan being built. What a fantastic sight to see after the bad energy hanging around the homestead of Georgia Pine. As always, it was a sheer pleasure to visit with them, the energy shifted dramatically to the positive when we got there. Sean and Ronnie were there from Flagstaff Support Group. I couldn't tell you how lovely it was to see friendly faces. Grandma and Grandpa were doing very well considering the harassment from the Hopi rangers they endure constantly. We sat and had lunch with them, laughed and joked about things and everything seemed well with the world again. Grandma's English was getting pretty good, I wish I could have said the same about my Dineh!

Grandpa told me he nearly cut his hand off with the chainsaw, and of course he wouldn't go to the hospital but instead fixed it with herbs himself. He called the medicine "dope." I kept laughing thinking someone had told him the wrong English, but apparently they have always called it dope. I was completely amazed to see the wound looking better than I've seen in any hospital, and he had full use of his hand. He was the most extraordinary man and I admired them both a great deal. He told me that his grandkids ask him to teach them about the plants, but he won't teach them because they like to eat them too much. I asked why they would eat them and he says because the plants make films in your head and it is dangerous. Obviously these healing plants are also hallucinogenic.

I love the way the Dineh describe things. Man I wish I could learn about the plants, though. Grandma still had her ragged cough. The doctors couldn't seem to find anything wrong with her lungs, but apart from that she was also doing very well. She sold all her crafts at the Christmas fair and had nothing really to sell us, which was a bummer for me though great for them. We bought the last few pieces she had anyways. Every trip I have been up there I have bought jewelry, and now sadly find I have given most of it away. I wonder who has it all and hope they still treat it as special. It might not be precious stones, but pine nuts and beads made on Big Mountain seem to be imbued with the elder's magical energy.

Grandpa was still concerned about the contaminated stone in his house. He told me some men had visited who told him they would come and help, but they never came back. Some other men brought up a Geiger counter and told him the rads measured 80. I'm not sure if he meant Ben and James, who had promised to come and help him, or if he meant other Indian people who had come and measured it. It's difficult to tell, as our language is limited and the Dineh speak about people differently. They don't remember names; they attribute names to them. To Grandma and Grandpa Alder I was the "daughter from Los Angeles." I felt very guilty about not helping more. I bet they never came back because it meant putting themselves in danger, or maybe, and as usual, lots of promises were made and never kept; promises made in the moment to make you feel good, but these same people find hard to return to once off the rez. I remember looking at him with such abject adoration; I had to stave off the tears that sprang up in my eyes. He glanced at me, smiled and turned away. In that moment, I saw the inner pain in the man's eyes, a man who had proudly built his own house with his bare hands with "special rocks" he had not been told were dangerous, and his beloved wife and family had lived in this house for years and still do. The family he had exposed to radiation. Devastating.

I was so reluctant to leave. I love them so much, but we had to visit others so off we went to see Grandma Eucalyptus and Ruby Willow. These two elders lived in a particularly remote canyon, which was very difficult to get to. It was hard to recognize the turn off even in good weather. In bad weather, it's unlikely one would ever make it out of there as the road in, like most "driveways," is a narrow dirt track but this one had sheer cliffs that drop away to the canyon bottom on one side. Grandma Eucalyptus was delighted to see the huge donation of food we brought, especially the baby food; they have a new two-month-old in the family. She said she hoped we would come back with more food in January. Her sons were happy to see some strangers; they thought we were tourists, which made us all laugh. I guess even tourists sometimes stumble upon them in that vast wilderness.

Next stop, Ruby Willow, who lived in a hogan not far from Grandma Eucalyptus. Ruby was another favorite of mine who was, unfortunately, sick with a bad cough. The nurse was hopefully coming to get her Monday to take her to the hospital. We left lots of fresh produce and cans of food for her, and I left some cash for medicine. At least some of her family was visiting to see how she was doing. I was bummed to miss her sister, who is blind, but we were so late already I trusted they would share, and we took off for LA. It was a stunning day for weather, and the ride was immensely enjoyable with Erica. Erica and Christina had switched cars. Stefan was driving Erica crazy because he didn't allow smoking in his car. These road trips are so long and intense that you have to find your right road buddy; otherwise it can all go horribly wrong, as well I knew. Erica and I chatted, chain-smoked, and drank way too much coffee, which appalled Stefan but what the hey, we had a great trip back. We arrived in LA very tired at about 2 am after many truck stop sandwiches on the road. I am so grateful for all the prayers of protection we had from friends in LA and on the rez. I felt them very strongly that weekend. I couldn't do without them or my great road companions. Over the years, my spiritual beliefs have grown and changed a lot. They continue to do so, but my core belief that everything is energy and that energy can be manipulated to help or hurt remains.

Black Mesa Meditation
Little Big Pine

Grandma, Grandpa, Nihima
Wind, blow this poem down the Navajo Road! -
Tell shell-white Moon my eyes to shine,
Let there be Light that way all night.

Grandma, Grandpa, Nihima –
Wind, blow this poem down the Navajo Road! –
Marry Mount Beautiful to my soul,
Let Beauty be that way in me.

Grandma, Grandpa, Nihima –
Wind, blow this poem down the Navajo Road! -
Keep good Medicine in my mind,
Let Spirit heal that way in time.

Grandma, Grandpa, Nihima –
Wind, blow this poem down the Navajo Road! -
Song-plant Big Mountain in my heart,
Let all Love thrive that way inside.

XVIII

Relocation Deadline January 27th, 2000

Rowan is someone I call a Goddess girlfriend from England who was always anxious for adventure. I call her my Goddess friend because there was a small group of us girls in London who fervently believed in the Earth as a Goddess. We met every week at Rowan's house, would divine on Tarot cards, drink tea, smoke, and generally wish for a more matriarchal world and endlessly complain about men. Rowan lived in a council flat in Islington with her daughter until it burned down. The council had to re-house her to a nicer flat, something she had wanted and waited years for. She was a photographer, and had decided to come out to the land with me during the relocation deadline to have an adventure, take photographs, and experience reservation life. I am not sure if it was the complete change from London that made her put up her resistance to the experience in the end, or the fact that her life had finally come to some kind of crisis, but the adventure for Rowan was not what she expected. Is it ever? Unfortunately, when people have lived hard lives and have not experienced a "spiritual awakening" for want of a better phrase, they are generally quite selfish, and selfishness is a hard taskmaster when you are on the rez. The shadow comes back to bite you, and so it did with Rowan.

Rowan and I must have finally left LA around 11 am on January 27th. The truck was packed to the brim with gear for a week's stay and a few boxes of donations. We were both very excited, and I was extremely happy to have some English company. I was starved for it in fact, and couldn't believe that Rowan was finally there, and we were getting ready to go. I left as much room as possible in the back of the truck so I could pick up some dog food from Plateau Lands veterinarians in Flagstaff. It was a pretty uneventful drive, which was a blessing in so many ways. We arrived in Flagstaff at night, and the temperature had dropped significantly. It was the middle of winter and snow lay on the ground. Before we did the final leg of the journey, which was always the most difficult because of the dark and how exhausted you get from driving for twelve hours, we stopped to eat at Denny's. Although I find Denny's to be a horrible restaurant chain, especially for a vegetarian, it is, on the other hand, easy to find and always open, so we loaded up on carbs and coffee for the final cold leg of the journey.

The lady we were picking up the dog food from lived down a small back road in a ranch style house, just on the other side of Flag. Luckily, her house was on our way, and she had given us great directions, so it wasn't too hard to find. Rowan and I made short work of loading up the animal food and started the last part of the drive to the mountain, always the hardest part. It was very cold that night, and we were layered up in all of our warm clothes. There was one part of the drive up to the mesa, which was dubbed, "Death Alley." The road was long and straight with dark pine trees lining the side and you can see many make-shift crosses surrounded by flowers dotted along the way. Too many drunk drivers on their way back to the rez decide to speed down this road and end up crashing into a tree. It's a sad sight, and really eerie in the middle of the night.

We finally got up to Morgaine's trailer around midnight. Mike Harris, (the new lawyer) and the two young trainee activist lawyers were asleep in the office, so we bedded down in Morgaine's trailer. It was way too cold to camp out. Of course, she talked all freakin night, mainly about Greystone and the possibility of them getting married, but things still were not good between them. I hate to say it, but I thought it was mainly wishful thinking on her part, as I couldn't see him leaving his family. I did feel really sorry for her though. Who hasn't been totally in love and the victim of every falsehood told? She would talk about the old traditions where one man could have more then one wife, but that was a very old way when perhaps jealousies were not a part of the Dineh life and all strove for harmony. It seems to create nothing but chaos now.

It was obvious Morgaine hadn't had a great love life. She was short of stature and not graced with outward beauty, but had lovely raven black hair, an overbite, glasses, and could talk the hind legs off a donkey. Greystone must have seemed to her the epitome of her knight in shining armor. He was tall, nice looking, and strong with jet-black hair. A man who cared about his people, the land, and what befell them, and worked hard to protect the elders. I really hoped if this didn't work out there was somebody else out there for her.

XIX

January 28, 2000

The next day we drove to Rocky Ridge Chapter House to attend Lisa Pine's meeting with some Swedish people, who had come over to lend their support. I still didn't trust Lisa much, but the Dineh are very forgiving of their own kind. They don't make judgments so there was nothing for it but to start working in coalition when needed. The lawyer Mike had a chance to speak to the gathered crowd for a while. I was getting bored, so went outside to find the Dineh teenagers I had met before: Sara, the beautiful but troubled daughter of Kevin Sycamore, and the two boys, Arthur and Percy, who always tried to act badly, but underneath had hearts of gold. The kids on the rez were all bored and frustrated. There was nowhere for them to go, no money to do anything, and nothing to do. Most of them hardly had any warm clothes or coats for the cold weather and spent their time walking around the rez trying to get a hold of some grass. I felt so bad for them. Later, we organized another meeting for Mike to talk legal stuff at the Anna Mae camp for the next day.

Mike and his crew, Peter and Amelia, had to meet somebody elsewhere so we went back to Big Mountain to pick up David Oak to interpret for us. We then met back up with the legal crew and headed off over to Coalmine Mesa to see Ruby Willow. Luckily, she was at home and welcomed us in. The stove in her hogan was burning really hot, so we all had to start peeling off layers. We were all bundled up in warm clothes, as it was still very cold outside. The heat really got to me, and as I was so tired from the long drive into the night I kept dozing off whilst Ruby recounted her story to Mike of how the BIA had been abusing her. She was such an amazing lady, diminutive but nonetheless a wonderfully strong woman. I can still recall the scene in her hogan so vividly: the lambs in the cage, the heat, Ruby standing, hands on hips, defiant, dark eyes glittering, declaring she was ready to go to court that she had testified in murder trials, and she was not scared. She told us how she had chased the BIA out of the canyon on horseback when they had come to impound her animals, which made us all laugh. What a picture! We stayed there so late listening to Ruby that we had to forego visiting the Alders, which was disappointing

XX

January 29, 2000

Christine and Stefan arrived late the previous night. They decided to sleep in their tent as the trailer was packed with people. We tried to persuade them not to because of the bitter cold, but they went ahead anyways. In the middle of the night, they woke everybody up and came to sleep in the trailer when they realized there was going to be no sleep for them in such freezing temperatures. I was so tired I crashed out quickly.

In the morning, after a quick breakfast we took off early for Star Mountain picking up Karen Samuels and Mary Goode on the way. I'd never been to Star Mountain before, as it was way past Second Mesa on the way to Winslow. We drove past a mountain that looked so like a breast, I decided to call it Nipple Mountain. Later on, I found out that was actually its name, or rather to be precise it was called Nipple Mesa, which made us all laugh. We spent the day at Star Mountain with Ivy, Lily, and Vera Clark taking testimonies from them and others including Jane Peters - for the legal case Mike was building. Rowan and I went outside to get some fresh air. One of the young men showed me which mountain was Star Mountain. It didn't look very much like a Star, so I said as much to the young man. He said that it probably did from the air, which of course raised the question of how did the Dineh, who have been earthbound sheepherders for decades, know it was shaped like a star from the air? There are many myths of alien visitors in this area, and the infamous Roswell isn't that far. Strange sightings and events become much more plausible the more time you spend on the rez. There was some inexplicable energy up there, as if things shifted slightly and the imagined became real.

As usual, Rowan was getting really bored, so went off for a horse ride with one of the Dineh. There were some other white supporters there. One girl wanted to show me some puppies. As I hugged the dogs the supporters made comments that they didn't touch the dogs after seeing them rolling in sheep shit. I laughed at them and said, "Well, I can always wash my hands; I do not care about that." I cannot imagine not pouring love into my hands and stroking those animals, they suffer so much. As we were admiring the puppies, one of the foolish white boys dropped one and it hurt its leg. They where being too careless for my liking and I told them to take it to the vet. One young man said he would. Later, the girl came up to me to tell me that the Dineh often didn't have the choice of taking their animals to the vets. I said I understood that perfectly well, but it was not the Dineh who dropped the puppy, it was the volunteer and if we fucked up then we should be prepared to help them out.

Who knows if the supporters understood, I just hoped they took care of it. I found them quite stupid and ignorant; they didn't look much like they minded being dirty themselves so I can't see why they minded a bit of sheep shit. I can't stand kids who quote Dineh culture at me; I had been there long enough and to make that excuse not to help an animal you have hurt is totally irresponsible. I doubt very much if they told the Grandmother they'd hurt one of her precious puppies and it is another one of my huge regrets that I didn't speak up to the Grandma or take it to the vet myself.

Mary had to go to work, so she asked me to take Karen home – oh boy, Grandma responsibility. Karen sang her sacred song before departing, and we drove the incredibly bad washboard road home. On the way, she pointed out a rainbow around the sun, saying it meant rain. Indeed it did, that night it snowed heavily. After dropping Grandma Karen off at her hogan, we drove to David Oak's to meet up with the others. Winter, Susan and Daisy turned up at David's, and we had a meeting/catch up session. There was a lot to talk about. We had yet to finalize exactly what we were going to do as a protest for the final relocation day. The BIA had threatened to show up armed and forcibly remove all the remaining resisters. Rowan was acting antsy all the time; she wasn't really into our discussion and couldn't understand why everything was taking so long! Nothing ever happened quickly on the rez, and no discussion was ever quick either. I couldn't seem to make Rowan understand that this wasn't London, and people on the rez took their time to discuss things and think about things. This was why we were there, not just to entertain ourselves.

Finally, we had to go as Rowan threatened to faint from lack of food. I knew she was hypoglycemic, so I wanted to get her back to the trailer and get some food in her before she passed out. We drove back to the trailer where Rowan then decided she was ok and would wait for dinner – go figure. That really annoyed me as I don't like being manipulated, and I was there specifically to help the elders for the relocation deadline, not to make sure Rowan had a jolly holiday. She had not stopped complaining about getting some weed to smoke since the day we had arrived. I had told her we could get some, and I was sure it would come about as it always did, but, as I had explained before, this wasn't London. I couldn't just call someone and have them drive by in a few hours to deliver. You just have to wait for the opportune moment and trust. I tried to explain that it would take a few days, so she should just hold on and be patient. She couldn't wait though, and it had become really irritating listening to her complain of having no weed when we were surrounded by people who barely had enough to live on and whose entire life was threatened. I couldn't figure out why she was being like this, but there are so many subtle energies that play with you on the mountain. They weave around, rubbing your emotions raw, exposing you to the bone; inciting chaos and amplifying whatever is inside of you. It is imperative to keep focused on your mission and keep powerful prayers around you at all times or fall foul to these negative influences, as so many did.

XXI

January 30th, 2000

In the morning, Rowan and Daisy wanted to get some pictures of the mine up close. I'd never actually been in to the mine, so I was up for the adventure. We took off early to achieve our subversive mission before the Anna Mae camp meeting with Mike. We couldn't find the road into the actual mine at first past the storage building; I nearly ran straight into security and had to tell Rowan to put her camera down as we spun a u-turn and fled. We finally found our way into the heart of the mine. It was the Christmas holidays still, so we were hoping not to run into too many people, and luckily the guard did not follow us.

I didn't realize how deep the mining went. We managed to get up one ramp to discover the hideous black open wound on our Mother Earth that was the coal mine. It was like something out of a futuristic horror movie. Black liquid oozed from the ground like pus from a septic wound; toxic smoke rose from the pools of liquid. It was a scene of raw carnage with the great Peabody cranes towering above the seam, ready to make their hideous surgery on the Earth once again. My crow friends, Magda and Dagda, flew with their cousins all around us. They started to caw loudly at me, a sign I had come to know that we needed to leave, and with a sickening feeling growing in all of our stomachs and spirits, we left the scene of Peabody's crime.

We were all deeply affected by the obscenity of what we had seen. I had to sing the prayer song just to calm my heart and keep my knees from wobbling out of their skin.

We drove to the Chevron station to gas up and take a breather from the awful negativity that pervaded our minds and spirits from what we had just witnessed. My spirit was in such an awakened state that seeing this oozing open wound on the Earth, what havoc people could wreak, and how foul a crime it was to our Goddess, was devastating to me.

On the way out of the mine even the truck started playing up, and I guessed that the dark spirits that abided in that mine had somehow entered my mechanical horse. I checked the fluids at the gas station but couldn't tell what was wrong; some mechanical mishap was definitely starting, though. The windscreen was steaming up and there was a faint sweet smell. We finally showed up at the meeting around 3 pm when it was well under way. Winter and Susan were supposed to have taken David to see Julia Butterfly Hill at Roberta Blackgoat's for breakfast, but he had decided to get drunk instead and had tried to get them to carry a gun in the car to protect his brother – sigh! Here we go with the drama. Protect Peter from what exactly was never determined.

Julia Butterfly Hill had just come down from a 738-day tree-sit in the ancient redwoods in protest of clear cutting and had brought a lot of attention to the issue of logging old growth. She was currently the golden child of environmentalism, so to have her up on the land meant a lot to people. It was the time when she still couldn't bear to wear shoes, and even though it was freezing on the ground she showed remarkable strength of character walking around barefoot.

Lisa was hosting a good meeting; lots of people showed up including Chuck, a young Dineh Man who had been at Georgia Pine's homestead when we brought Fox 11 with us. Also there were the Behanies who lived in LA. They were what was considered "the bad family," and had an awful reputation for attacking the elders and stealing money. There were even rumors that they would, or had gone, as far as murder. Well, they showed up but didn't cause too much of a problem. Winter and Susan talked to Lisa about them, and she told them that the Behanies did not represent the Dineh people on Big Mountain, so we did have the authority to stop them asking for donations at our Big Mountain benefit gigs.

The plan was to go with Peter Oak and Julia Butterfly to see the elders at Hotevilla, but as usual with any good plan on Big Mountain, chaos ensued. Peter took off with his new 'wife' (some Asian lady who had married Peter for unknown reasons) in someone's SUV. We couldn't find David Crouch or JQ, and Morgaine took forever to get it together. We lost Peter entirely, but decided to go and see Blue Star and Len at Hotevilla to ask them to come for a photo shoot at the HPL fence line for the deadline event. As we sat in Len's house explaining to him, he was clearly not impressed with our plan to cut the fence symbolically bringing the tribes together at a press conference. Blue Star was cool with the concept and he would come with us. Len said he was too busy with the upcoming Bean Dance to attend our deadline photo call, so we took off to try and catch up with the Peace Walk at Red Rock Chapter House. Peter Oak and Julia Butterfly never made it to Hotevilla. We found Julia at the community center in Red Rock with the Peace Walkers, forty to fifty Buddhists who were all walking for peace along with some other volunteers. The chapter house was crowded with very tired people. A man named Bahee was organizing it and he told everyone that the route was going to change and no one was to question that decision. Morgaine took great exception to this announcement especially as that would mean the walk would totally miss Cactus Valley and the entire mine area. I think most people were unaware of the politics or the underlying manipulations going on so didn't think much of it.

We ate, visited, and I found a kitten in the bathroom some hippies had lost from their van. Daisy and Paula decided to walk with the Buddhists, so we left them there and made plans with Julia Butterfly for the press conference the next day. Outside it had started to snow softly. Rowan had met a man called Marshall at the meeting, a good-looking Dineh, who flirted with just about everyone, but he had managed to impress her. Rowan complained about everything again and then we drove back to the trailer in the snow. It is amazing how much apparent quietude comes over a land when snow falls. Perhaps it's that each individual snowflake has its own design, and that makes it incredibly magical. The drive home was just that: magical, and thankfully not too hazardous.

XXII

January 31st, 2000

We woke to a white land covered in heavy snowfall, a winter snow deep and pure. I felt bad for the puppy that lived under Morgaine's trailer, so I put down an extra blanket, which made little difference. As Julia Butterfly was a doubtful show because of the traveling conditions, we had group discussions on what to plan and what we could hope for at tomorrows deadline. JQ's strategic activist mind came in very useful here. We endlessly went around the topic of the press conference whilst Morgaine interjected, saying we should cancel the entire show because nobody would travel in this kind of weather. I tried to get her to pull up the weather report on line, but that was laughed at. If we knew how long the storm would last, I ventured, we would have an idea if it was just a flurry or set to snow us in, but nobody wanted to listen. We finally came up with the simplest of plans: get Blue Star, who would represent the Hopi, and David Oak and/or some Grandmothers representing the Dineh, to meet at one of the fence lines and shake hands across it for a photo op. This would symbolically show there was no trouble between the two tribes, and possibly get them to cut the fence.

The only thing now left to do was to venture out in the snow to accomplish the task. Winter and Susan's car was out of the question as they had a Pontiac. A regular car wouldn't make it across the dirt roads, which by now would either be slush or inches deep in snow. My truck was still playing up, the strange smell lingered in the cab and the windscreen kept misting up, but we thought we'd be all right with the snow chains on. We had to keep the windows open a bit, but if we bundled up we'd be fine. We all stepped outside in the snow to commit to the plan when a large white diesel truck pulled up and our knight in shining armor arrived in the form of Jessie, his dog Ziggy, and his fantastic truck. What a sight it was, completely heaven sent. We were all awestruck that he had just pulled up to the trailer just when we needed a large truck built for back roads. He introduced himself and his dog, and I think was a bit overwhelmed with the reception he received from us. He had been following Julia Butterfly and had tracked Susan down to get more info, lucky for us he found her. After introductions, we kidnapped Jessie and his truck for the day and took off to round up people for the press conference. We hadn't gone far past David Oak's when my truck started to reek a toxic fume, and smoke began whispering out of the vents, so I pulled over. David and Jessie inspected the engine and said my heater cone must have burned out, so we drove it back to David's and left it there for the day. Jessie said he could fix it later. It turned out he was a skilled mechanic as well; I thought I might make him an offer of marriage! Rowan and I jumped in the back of Jessie's wagon, and I finally found myself relaxing enough to enjoy the ride as we slipped and slid down the snow-covered road. Rowan just wouldn't sit still, and ended up banging her head quite hard on the roof of the truck as we ran over one rather large bump in the road, which didn't go down well.

We visited Jane, Esther, and Kevin Sycamore and Karen Samuels, and then onto Hotevilla. We called on Blue Star, and then down to the Kikmongwe's house to see if we could persuade any other Hopi to come to our press conference tomorrow. He said again they were preparing for the Bean ceremony, which was going to be early this year and so couldn't attend. Len also said that the sacred bundles that the Hopi and Dineh exchanged were not being taken care of properly whatever that meant. I kinda thought he'd given us his answer the day before, but Winter wanted to try again, so we did. As we waited outside, some of the Hopi kids came up to us to see what was going on. It was a slightly tense situation, they had been drinking and were half concealing metal pipes in their hands. God love em! They started to try and chat us up! Either they couldn't tell how old Rowan and I were in the dark, or were just out for some white tail. Either way, sometimes growing up in the city comes in handy when confronting hormonal teens concealing weapons. We handled it with as much good humor as possible and finally got back to the trailer late again, only to find no one had cooked. We were extremely tired, hungry, and starting to get really grumpy.

XXIII

February 1st, 2000

The weather cleared up, and even though it was cold the sun shone for us. We met with a bunch of press, representatives from the Dineh and Blue Star from Hotevilla, and completed what we thought was a very successful press conference at the fence line. We found out Grandmother Karen Samuels had been given the wrong info and had set herself up at another place on the fence line, so we all ran over there to do some more press. She was not impressed with us, and we politely sat to hear her admonishments. We all then went over to Roberta Blackgoat's house for the gathering of the Peace Walkers. It was fantastic to see so many people, but it was very cold outside and good to start getting back to the trailer. It was quite the hair-raising drive back down Roberta's road, as it is probably one of the worst on the rez. I don't know how some of the cars got up there. The dirt road was so narrow and steep it seemed like the truck would tip over, and we had to hold on for dear life. Susan and Winter had an especially challenging drive in their vehicle as they had a tall van, so it nearly did tip over and of course Winter took the opportunity to scream at everyone else whose fault she thought it was. Creech, Susan and I then took Blue Star back to Hotevilla.

XXIV

February 2nd, 2000

The next day we went back over to Roberta's land to hang out at the gathering and pretty much didn't do anything all day. The amazing Jessie fixed my truck, and we found that the press conference at the fence line had made the front pages, so we were very happy. We had another hairy drive out of Roberta's, but everyone eventually made it.

XXV

February 3rd, 2000

Rowan decided to stay on the mountain as long as she could. I didn't blame her, but that left me without a back up driver or companion for the twelve-hour drive home, which was not cool. Luckily, another activist, Paula, needed a ride, so I drove back to LA with her. Extremely tired, we made it. Home at last, I had a wonderful hot shower and fell exhausted into a warm bed.

XXVI

The Ill Fated Thanksgiving Run 2000

Four cars and nine people including me, Susan from ARC, Stefan from the Santa Monica Farmers Market, Winter, Joe and Roseanne, Lance, Sun, Joe's friend Jack, and Ronnie Orenna (singer activist from LA), all left for BM from my house on Thursday morning before Thanksgiving day. We were supposed to leave at 6 am, but Joe's dog sitter didn't arrive, and Winter, Susan and Stefan were late due to some conflict that nobody wanted to talk about. We finally set off at 8 am with Stefan, Winter and Susan leading the way in their vehicle. Winter had already started the dissent and was apparently arguing about which route to take, so Stefan, who was driving them, got thoroughly confused and lost sight of the caravan. After watching Stefan's car change lanes numerous times and eventually losing them, we decided it would be best if we switched around, so Joe and Rosanne took the lead and Sun, Lance and I pulled up the rear to catch any stragglers. We finally all got it together. Joe and Rosanne were pulled over by the cops for changing drivers on the side of the road but didn't get a ticket or anything, so that was ok. We ended up taking a more southern route than normal via Phoenix, as Winter and Susan had taken it previously and were convinced that it was much quicker. The caravan pulled up at a gas station just outside Phoenix. Winter wanted some batteries and DV film so she could film the sacred sites up on BM as part of a protection plan she had in mind. Trying to find DV film on a holiday weekend was not a good idea, everywhere was closed but stubborn she is, so she took off anyway to try. As the rest of us sat at the gas station waiting, the clock ticked on and on, and she didn't come back for three hours. The whole group was extremely frustrated and angry about being made to wait that long. We had discussed leaving, but felt that if something had happened to them no one would be able to help. Then we talked about splitting the group up, but as only Winter, Stefan and I knew the way onto the rez that didn't seem like a good idea either so there was nothing left for it but to wait. It's a hard, long drive, and this delay would put us on the rez at about 2 am when no one would be awake. The route via Phoenix had not turned out to be short at all either, so we were already later then we wanted to be. Winter's saboteur antics were starting to put me over the edge. When she got back to the garage, she refused to apologize for making us wait, and didn't seem to see any problem at all. We were all furious at her.

We finally headed to Flagstaff with angry energy already brewing in the group. We saw some elk on the way up who bounded across the road directly in front of us; wish I'd known more about the meaning of elk medicine. They were huge, and we were so lucky not to hit them. We rounded up again in Flagstaff to gas up, and things started getting really hairy as Winter decided to tie up a peyote drum at the gas station, appalling everyone. Apart from the fact that it was very inappropriate to put together a drum used in ceremony at a public gas station, it was delaying us even more. Our stops were getting too long and too many. Winter, Joe and Rosanne had been eating peyote and Susan was stoned which all made for very "interesting," challenging and chaotic energy, something I could well do without.

Incredibly, when we left the gas station, Winter announced over the walkie-talkie that she hadn't, in fact, put any gas in her truck so we would have to stop again! I was totally pissed of with her at this point. The frustration continued to mount, as by now we were four-and-a-half hours behind schedule and having to stop again! I felt that Winter was deliberately causing aggravation for some mad reason. As we left the gas station again, Winter took the lead as she insisted she knew the way up to Hotevilla. We were heading up to Blue Stars first who always made us welcome and had a second house in the village we usually could stay in. I hadn't driven that way in a while so I felt my sense of direction might be hazy, especially in the dark. What a mistake that was! Winter sailed past the turning onto the mesa, and I didn't realize until after a few miles down the road. We were going via Loup, so there was another road we could take but again we missed the 2 turn off, then Winter turned her walkie-talkie off so I couldn't get through to tell her we were again going the wrong way. When finally she pulled over, I was unsure of the way but said that the 2 was the road we should be taking. Winter was again completely convinced the 2 was a bad road, mainly dirt, so we continued as I was by then very confused by her disinformation. It turned out that was another huge mistake; she had taken us the long way round by way of Second Mesa tacking on about another forty-five minutes to the already long journey. It was really late, and everyone was overly tired and annoyed. I don't know what had gotten into her, apart from peyote of course, but she was clearly being obstreperous and divisive.

As we were finally on the approach to First Mesa, Winter suddenly turned a hard right off the main road onto the Pinon dirt road, and started heading across the mountain to Pinon! At that point, my truck companions and I had had enough;

it was early hours of the morning, we were tired, hungry and cold. We stopped the caravan and decided to take the lead the rest of the way in, something I should have done long ago. Winter, however, became furious that we refused to follow her, but luckily I had driven the Pinon road before and knew there was nothing for miles and miles, just dirt road. We would have put everyone in serious jeopardy not to mention not going anywhere but the middle of the mesa for hours. Besides, it was clear by then she was in some kind of psychosis and we had been patient with her long enough.

Finally, exhausted and cold, we arrived at Blue Star's house at about 1:00 am, which was 2:00 am mountain time. Unsurprisingly, we couldn't rouse Blue Star without waking the neighbors. Usually he would hear us coming and come outside, but there was no sign of any life, so I was elected to walk into the village to see if he was at his other house. No one else knew where he lived. Winter had rolled up her windows, refusing to talk to anyone and was busy preparing to sleep! After dragging us all around the mesa half the night, keeping people waiting for hours, and turning off her CB, she was now not giving a fuck about anyone else and where we were all going to sleep. It was freezing outside with a light snow on the ground and it would be way too cold to sleep in the cars. Well, I highly doubted anyone could actually sleep in that cold; you would just be dozing, hoping not to freeze to death and at that point I was hoping the woman would freeze to fucking death.

I trudged into the village by myself, scared at first and then enjoying the chance to stretch my legs under a canopy of an inky, black sky scattered with brilliant stars. I couldn't find Blue Star's village house for a while because of all the construction going on; which was in itself incredibly strange. The village was so quiet, but I could see electric lights on in some houses, something I had never, EVER seen up there before. Having electricity in Hotevilla was against what all the traditional Hopi stood for. They had fought vociferously to stop sewage lines being dug in the village for indoor toilets and trenches being dug for power lines. This would have disturbed the sacred bundles that had long ago been buried in the Four Directions around the village.

I stood in the center of the village trying to get my bearings and asked for guidance. I turned around and looked down to see I was standing on a sewer drain, in Hotevilla!! I couldn't believe it, right in the middle of the village. It was like an ominous warning that everything here had changed. That I would walk to a spot and find myself standing directly on the one thing that the traditional elders had fought so hard against was like the sign of doom. I was now convinced it was the end of Hotevilla; the struggle was lost, and Hotevilla no longer the sacred shrine it once was. The world had turned upside down, and the twins had moved from the axis, just as the Hopi prophecy predicted. The myth says there are two warrior brothers each guarding the North and South Pole. The brothers keep the world in balance and when they move the "Fourth World," the world we currently live in, will shift.

One of the village dogs suddenly appeared to show me where Blue Star lived, but it was as if the whole thing was staged, like I had for a moment entered a different dimension. I was meant to see the sewer drain, meant to understand that it was over for Hotevilla, it was lost to the traditional ways. I wondered what happened to the sacred bundles. The traditional Hopi elders had not wanted the bulldozers to come into the village to dig sewers in case they disturbed them. And there I was, standing on a drain.

There was no one in at the village house, and it wasn't a good idea to be hanging alone in the village at night, so I walked back to the trucks. We decided to camp in the cars for a while until Blue Star woke up. Just as I was dozing off someone knocked at the window. It was Blue Star, bless his heart! I guess we had finally made enough noise, and he had gotten up. I had to wake Stefan and get him to drive us to the village to start a fire for us in the other house, then we came back to get the others. Joe's car wouldn't start because it was so cold and they didn't want to walk the five minutes to the house, so we left them there and gratefully cozied up in the house by the fire. At that point, I didn't care if Winter and her horrendous companions all froze to freaking death.

The next day Blue Star's wife, Pearl, needed to use the house to bake for a hair - washing ceremony, so Blue Star took us to the field house in the morning. It was at his family's cornfield. I had never been there, so I was very excited to be going to what the Hopi considered their most sacred place, the cornfield. Blue Star wanted our help to clean out the house, so we started to do that when a huge fight erupted between Winter and me as we were sweeping. It started over nothing, but my patience was done, and I had enough of the chaos and drama of her energy that weekend. The fight snowballed, as once I blow up there is no stopping me. Winter got really upset and started to cry, and it ended with me, Sun, Blue Star, Stefan and Susan leaving to deliver supplies in Hotevilla. We had Sage with us, which is fantastic as she always had such joyful energy. Apparently, the drama continued after I left. I had upset Winter, and she was busy trying to vindicate herself and justify her actions to the remaining group. Joe apparently placated her by saying I was just trying to hurt her. No shit! She was lucky I hadn't punched her. Winter's psychosis had tried to kill us all the past night. But of course she was in total denial about this because she had eaten peyote and, to her, this made her right. The whole emotional drama was ridiculous and a pure example of how human's shit gets in the way of working together on issues.

At this point, everyone was fed up, so nothing really got resolved. Winter, Joe, and Roseanne left to go over to BM, and thankfully we didn't see them again that weekend. In fact, it would be years until I would see and speak to Winter again. It is really hard for me to forgive such downright craziness when other people's safety is at risk. Life suddenly got easier as a fresh breeze blew through all of us. We got back to discover Lance had fixed the house door, Ronnie had cleaned up, and who knew what Jack was doing but didn't care. We chilled out for the remaining day, fixing things as best we could. Nothing was flowing properly quite yet because of Winter's chaotic energy, but things were starting to settle down. Blue Star's dad's picture was stuffed into one of the broken windows. It was a great picture of him standing in the doorway of the cornfield house with these huge glasses on and a straw hat. Jack cooked curry, which was far too spicy and practically inedible, but we didn't mind too much and just tried to enjoy.

I found a typewriter in the field and recounted the story of the elders typing the Techqua Ikachi papers in secret, probably in that very cornfield. The Techqua Ikachi papers were a series of forty-four newsletters written by the Hopi traditional elders during the 1970's, in what would turn out to be the final days of their resistance to the onslaught of modernization. Then I found the wide-brimmed straw hat Grandpa Kootsie was wearing in the photo, so I wore it for a while. Strange how he still felt so present, his piercing eyes behind huge thick glasses in his photo scrutinizing us from the spirit world. Sage was hysterically funny all night and kept us laughing, what great medicine. She was totally wired on sugar. In the morning I made us breakfast, and we cleared out to take Sage home. I had to run some errands for Blue Star and then we were off to Grandma and Grandpa Alder's homestead. Clearly, I hadn't been over there in quite some time because I missed the turn off and ended up at Ruby Willow's turning, so we turned around and headed back. Later we figured we should have gone to Ruby's first as we missed her later. I should know to go with the flow by now on Big Mountain!

We got back to the Alder's house and secured our place for the night in their hogan. Susan had bought a turkey, which Grandpa put in a fire pit in the ground to cook. We did some errands and packed off with the Alder's grandkids to visit Ruby. I always loved it when the kids opted to ride with us for an adventure. Ruby wasn't in unfortunately, so we set about unloading some supplies. Lance, Jack, and Stefan cut a bunch of wood for her. We chased the sheep around for a bit, trying to put them in the coral, but just succeeded in exercising them and ourselves. We left as the sun was setting. Ruby's canyon was not a good place to be in the dark. The dirt roads aren't even roads; they were just tracks where previous car wheels had been. We made it back to the Alder's around 6 pm and cooked up a big dinner for everyone. We sat and talked for a while and then hit the sack. In his wonderfully gracious, hospitable way Grandpa had lit a fire and bought us some water; they were so wonderful, I love them so much. The new hogan was a great to sleep in, just to lie back on the soft sand and gaze up at the eight-sided roof. Through the hole in the top, I could see the stars. It was such a different energy now since we had parted company with Winter and the others. You couldn't help but just chill out when you're in the presence of the Alders. I miss them terribly now - such good people, I deeply regret not spending much more time with them, but youthful naivety doesn't warn you how quickly time goes and how precious it is. Never wait to do the things you want to do, my Ma says, and boy is she right. After some storytelling, we eventually went to sleep. I wanted to get up early and help out before we left. The next morning, the boys helped cut down a tree for firewood and the girls cleaned up the kitchen, made breakfast, and fed the lambs.

I sat and spun yarn with Grandma for a while. I could cry just thinking about it now. She didn't want me to go, and I didn't want to. I'm not sure why I never just chose to stay. Some kind of fear I guess stopped me. They needed help in December so we would have to try and figure that out. We left around midday, and visited Blue Star to finish business. He said he would mail us some things to sell. He gave me some Techqua Ikachi papers to photocopy and send back. I took the caravan to see the Prophecy Rock on the way out as a fitting end to visiting that amazing land and people. The journey home was smooth and fast. We arrived back in LA around 10:30 pm. It was always hard to come back after the relative wild and peaceful times spent on Big Mountain. There's a long incline on the freeway you hit just as you're coming into LA where you can see the city spread out before you in an endless field of lights. It's such a shock to the system after being somewhere with no light pollution, no electricity, and it strikes you. These beautiful people, an entire culture and way of life are dying so we can light our houses in such an obscenely wasteful way. Every time I flick a switch I think of them and thank them.

For years now the Indigenous People's of this planet have been warning us that we humans are creating climate change with our destructive ways. There was a time when the Hopi prophecy was spoken about in future tense but no longer. Climate change is here, and if we do not take drastic action now it will mean the end of the fourth world. The world we now live in.

Little did I know that the strange Thanksgiving run would be the last time I fully experienced Big Mountain as that time faded away from me. In the coming years, I had to say goodbye to many precious things in my life and all those took their toll. My Father died of cancer the next year, swiftly followed by my dear friend Kent Holladay, a Cherokee man who had shown me the wisdom of his Indian ancestors through so many confusing times. My dear mechanical horse, my little old truck that had carried me safely through all these adventures and held so many memories in her inanimate frame, was totaled in a car wreck. My Uncle Steve, my Auntie Gloria, Claudia, Justine, my brother-in-law Paul and my dearest soul sister, Snowdeer all passed from this life into the next from the ravages of cancer and to them I dedicate this tale.

In great physical pain from the car wreck that totaled my dear little truck, and with the broken heart of betrayal, I turned away to follow a different path, as the Creator seemed to wish. Not because, as rumors spreading from David Oak would have it, we got what we wanted and then left, but because I turned to tend to my own family, who were in need of me then and I of them. It became apparent that whatever energy had kept our little group safe and blessed was no longer available to me on the mountain, it was time to move on. As time passed, and my body and spirit healed from the toxins it had absorbed on Big Mountain, my focus changed. Again I took up the cause closest to my heart, the plight of the animal kingdom, and the evil abuse that is being visited upon them every second of every day by the human race.

XXVII

For The Love of The Earth
Summer Crystal Crow

I found out that Grandpa Huc Alder passed over. I don't know when it happened I just know that he died from cancer.

I recall my times with him vividly and mourn his passing. Another good one leaves us. One of the good ones, one of the few genuine "Hopi". This is meant not in the sense that he was Hopi - he wasn't even Dineh - but he had a good heart and shone like a beacon in the darkness.

I remember the first time I met Grandma and Grandpa Alder. We arrived in the dark. The house was dark because they didn't have any oil left for their lamps or batteries for the flashlights. He was dressed in his overalls, and Grandma sat in the corner beneath a ceiling that was falling down. Insulation hung down over her head as she coughed. We were all pained in our hearts, all of us who were visiting vowed to do something about their pitiful situation.

In the months, years that followed, we did. Huc finally received some money from fighting in the war. Not the Vietnam War, mind; the Second World War. He bought supplies to mend his house even though that was illegal at the time.

I remember painting the wall next to him as he told me about the 'special rocks" and the uranium mine they came from. I recall vividly the look in his eyes as he shared the story of collecting those special rocks to build his family house with and when he realized they were "hot" rocks.

I remember standing in the back of this truck, dumping stuff we had taken out of the house. It was just him and me. He told me how everyone was so surprised and wondered why he had so many friends who all came over to help them. He was so proud that he had that.

I remember him telling me about the ceremonies they would have in the hogan. The remarkably beautiful new hogan he built. How humble he was. He said he wasn't a medicine man because he could never remember all the songs and how he laughed about it. He was more medicine man then anyone I've ever met. Humble and beautiful with those piercing grey eyes.

Grandma told me about some supporters who had tried to sleep with Grandpa. I couldn't understand how women could be so disrespectful. Here was this beautiful couple, obviously fiercely in love and some white woman comes along and tries to bed an eighty-year-old man in front of his wife. How pathetic is that!

I can't tell you how much my heart hurts to know we've lost another one. Another old one, one that knew so much, So many plants, so much medicine. It reminds me that time is of the essence. Moments are fleeting, and you should never wait because the moment will pass from this world and never be there again.

Aho mitukeoyisin Grandpa Alder.
With deep respect.
May your journey be a good one. May the Goddess bless your wife until she returns home to you.

I hear HER coming. HER thunderous footsteps shake the ground.

A warrioress sent from the Mother to wield such power that will break those stone hearts of men and make them weep like the children they have slain upon this sacred ground. Their tears will give life to the trees. Thus will she wreak her terrible revenge and make us remember HER name!

Dedicated to the elders that have passed:
Roberta Blackgoat
John Babbit Lane
Huc Greyeyes
Pauline Whitesinger

Wake up!
You must wake up now,
The time for sleep is over.
When you wake, it won't be pretty but wake you must.

www.ingramcontent.com/pod-product-compliance
Lightning Source LLC
Chambersburg PA
CBHW032035290426
44110CB00012B/813